Echoes of slavery

Voices from South Africa's past

For Andrew, David and Malcolm

With love

Echoes of slavery

Voices from South Africa's past

Jackie Loos

david philip

First published in 2004 in southern Africa by
David Philip Publishers, an imprint of New Africa Books (Pty) Ltd,
99 Garfield Road, Claremont 7700, South Africa
www.newafricabooks.co.za

ISBN 0-86486-661-5

Cover and text design: Fresh Identity
Project manager: Karen van Eden
Editor: Angela Briggs
Typeset in 9pt (Stone Serif) by Fresh Identity
Printed and bound by
ABC Press, Cape Town

Contents

Preface

THIS IS NOT A history book – it is a collection of true stories, each chosen to illuminate a particular facet of Cape slavery in its mature form. British slavery has been seen as a period of erosion, but the hardship and loss of dignity endured by those in bondage changed little between 1658 and 1834. Although some of the incidents are well known, others are trivial enough to allow us to catch a glimpse of the everyday realities of the past. I have chosen to concentrate on the last 30 years of slavery because it places the least distance between Cape slaves and their modern descendants. Chrisje of the Cape's horror at the prospect of having her hair cut as a punishment in 1831 is easier to comprehend than the probable state of Valentijn of Madagascar's mind when he was sold for 80 wagon loads of firewood in 1689.

Much of the information was gleaned from previously untapped primary and secondary sources in the Cape Town Archives Repository and the National Library of South Africa. Professional historians seldom have time to digress, and it has been my pleasure to linger over individual stories and search for corroborating details in other documents. I have limited my research to privately-owned urban and agricultural slaves – the overwhelming majority at the Cape – and I have excluded the government slaves housed at the VOC Slave Lodge in the Heerengracht, whose numbers dwindled steadily until 1827, when the last few were emancipated.

Most of these sketches have previously appeared as weekly columns in the *Cape Argus* under the banner 'The Way We Were', which looked at the history of Cape Town's previously marginalised underclasses. The scope has since been broadened to include adjacent parts of the Western Cape. When the series started in 1999, I was under the impression that, apart from fairly full criminal records, very few slave and free black stories had survived, but it soon became apparent that I was wrong. From 1806, when the British occupied the Cape for the second time, to the day when freedom was proclaimed in 1834, hundreds of illiterate slaves and ex-slaves (known officially as 'free blacks') addressed the authorities on subjects that were of vital interest to them.

Slaves complained to the fiscal, the courts and the Slave Protectors in increasing numbers in their quest for redress, justice and manumission. Free blacks caused letters and memorials to be written on their behalf by notaries (persons with some legal training) on a wide variety of topics. While it is true that these are filtered voices, translated into English from the Cape Dutch vernacular and re-worded in accordance with official phraseology, they often throb with barely suppressed indignation, anxiety or remorse.

The selective manner in which history was previously taught in our schools has led to a surprising degree of amnesia among South Africans about their slave origins. In the United States of America and Australia, slave and convict genealogies are regarded as marks of validation, if not distinction, but many of the descendants of Cape slaves ignore the richness of their pre-emancipation heritage. Slave women were the guardians of this legacy. They were renowned for their skill as domestics, nursery maids, cooks, washerwomen and seamstresses. They were intimately connected to the families they served, to the extent that they often suckled white infants, provided sexual services to male members of the household and nursed the sick and the dying. Numerous white families have slave ancestors in their genealogies, and it is time for them to acknowledge this with pride rather than with shame.

Prior to the 1990s, South Africans seldom acknowledged that slave skills and labour were crucial to fashioning the distinctive Cape heritage that attracts multitudes of international tourists today. Slaves constructed the basic infrastructure of the city, established the thriving fruit, wine, grain and fishing industries and built the stately Cape Dutch houses that have become national treasures. The exotic flavour they brought to our language, religion, culture and cuisine can be traced back more than ten generations.

Thanks are due to Michael Morris and Vivien Horler of the *Cape Argus* for giving me a platform, and to several local historians for their encouragement. I owe a large debt of gratitude to the staffs of the Cape Town Division of the National Library of South Africa and the Cape Town Archives Repository for their unfailing patience and courtesy. I particularly value the response of my namesake Jackie Goliath, a lively informal parking attendant, who called out: 'I like to read your history stories!' as I passed her beat in Queen Victoria Street at the beginning of my newspaper career. She is still a regular reader, and her infectious enthusiasm has made it all worth while.

Because so few images of individual slaves have come down to us, the illustrations have been chosen to show various aspects of life at the Cape during the last decades of slavery.

Vredehoek
January 2004

Introduction

MOST TRAVEL WRITERS WHO described life at the Cape during the seventeenth and eighteenth centuries were European men who chose to regard slavery as a necessary evil. On arrival, they found an immature and inefficient economy dependent on plentiful supplies of free land and coercible labour, and they were generally biased in favour of the bluff, hospitable burghers they met, unaware of – or unmoved by – the tension and brutality that characterised their relationships with their slaves. These male Christian voices have tended to overpower the cadences of the handful of women and the occasional Oriental who commented on Cape society during the slave era. Fortunately, their books have survived to speak for them.

Jemima Kindersley (1741 to 1809), a young Englishwoman who was accompanying her husband to Bengal, has left an interesting record of a summer spent at the Cape when Ryk Tulbagh was governor.[1] She was 23 when she arrived in Table Bay in November 1764, and she liked Cape Town immediately, particularly its regularity and neatness.

She noticed that most of the servants were slaves from the East Indies, and wrote: 'What seems extraordinary is that they do not learn to talk Dutch, but the Dutch people learn their dialect, which is called Portuguese, and is a corruption of that language ...' Her description of the violent passions that sometimes caused slaves to 'run amok' and inflict injury indiscriminately, was testimony to the anguish and hopelessness that slavery induced. She was horrified by the harsh punishments that followed: 'The execution ... was the most cruel that could be invented by the art of man: a lingering death upon the rack, with the application of burning instruments in a manner too shocking to repeat.'

The smallpox epidemic of 1755 was still a topic of conversation during Jemima's visit, and she wrote: 'The small pox when it happens amongst them, which is perhaps once in ten, or seven years, is a most dreadful calamity; the devastation it makes exceeds belief; whole families, parents, children and slaves are sometimes carried off by it; it spreads itself all over the country, and people shut themselves up from their neighbours, to escape the pestilence.' The colonists blamed the climate for the high mortality, but she attributed it to their ignorance in managing the disease and their poor physical condition. She found the white inhabitants 'mostly fat gross people' as a result of a diet that included 'a vast quantity of grease and butter', and she thought them extremely indolent, for 'they are not in this country active, but the labour is left entirely to the slaves'.

Lady Anne Barnard (1750 to 1825), the aristocratic, worldly-wise wife of the colonial secretary, Andrew Barnard, had no direct experience of slavery until she arrived at the Cape in 1797, but she deplored its negative influence.[2] She believed that many colonists feared their slaves, and she ascribed their solicitude for slave women during childbirth to their fear of losing valuable property. 'The loss of Sophy might be the loss of 150 Rixdollars – without including 20 Rixdollars or so for the kint [child].' Despite these insights, she tended to stereotype slaves as carefree, irresponsible, incompetent and immoral, and she failed to recognise that the pilfering she found so irritating was a surreptitious form of resistance.

Although her staff frequently disappointed and exasperated her, she continued to take an interest in them. Sensing this perhaps, January, the government slave who took care of her poultry – 'an innocent, harmless lad' – accosted her at her official country residence 'Paradise' one day. 'Cleyne hunders,' he said, smiling broadly, and beckoned her Ladyship to follow him through the bush to share his wonder. There, in the root of an old tree, he showed her a hollow in which 'a poor hen had deposited her eggs, 13, and had hatched already eight chickens, the prettiest little infants ever were seen ...'

According to Lady Anne, some Dutch ladies of her acquaintance were critical of her tolerance. 'In particular I see I am reckoned very wrong for not turning out of the room the slaves of my guests who like to stand at the door and see the dancing. Now, though I don't much like the smell of the slaves' oil [presumably the coconut oil they used on their hair] and would rather they were not there, if the mistress chooses to bring a slave to wait on her, I do not choose to turn her out. I wish to make all happy after their own way, and I do not wish to make a very few happy in the exclusion or mortification of others.'

In June 1799, Lady Anne met a handsome Asiatic stranger at a Cape dinner party. Abu Talib ibn Muhammad Khan (1752 to *c*.1806), also known as Mirza Abu Taleb Khan, was the son of a Persian nobleman.[3] Born in India, he enjoyed princely favour until the 1790s, when he lost his influential position during a power struggle. Being temporarily unoccupied, he decided to visit Europe with his friend Captain Richardson, who acted as his interpreter while he learned to speak English. Their tour lasted from 1799 to 1803. Abu Talib kept a journal, written in Persian, of his 'many tedious journeys', which was translated into English and published in 1810. It was said to be the first time that 'the genuine opinions of an

1. Cape slaves reaping cereal crops while their owners enjoy a life of luxury and ease. This idealised late eighteenth century mural representing summer was commissioned by Johan Bernhard Hoffman for the homestead at Libertas, Stellenbosch. Hoffman's grandson, born in 1772, was a notary who wrote detailed and affecting petitions on behalf of slaves and free blacks.

Asiatic, respecting the institutions of Europe' had appeared in the English language.

The travellers spent the first winter at the Cape, which had fallen to the British in 1795. Lady Anne, a compulsive diarist who 'wished every hour three, that I might have leisure to say all I could', was fascinated by this exotic visitor, whom she called Khan Saijb. When he called at her rooms in the Castle one morning, wearing a very fine purple and white striped turban and graceful robes of cloth of gold, she hurried to meet him in her 'powdering gown', being unwilling to keep him waiting while she changed.

She admired his fine spirited countenance, full of fire and intelligence, and his sallow complexion 'which serves to give the greater lustre to his white teeth'. They were soon on comfortable terms, and she warned him of the attention he would receive in England, particularly from women. The Persian, a man of refinement and culture, had already noticed that Cape girls, unlike their overweight mothers, were hand-

2. Cape Town seen from the ramparts of the Castle during the First British Occupation. It shows the Great Barracks (originally a hospital), the walled execution place where criminals were hanged or flogged, and the main road connecting the town to the interior. Section of a panorama by Lady Anne Barnard, c. *1798.*

some, sprightly and good-natured, but he was embarrassed by their boisterous behaviour and lack of decorum. He wrote: 'Although I was ignorant of the Dutch language, and could not converse with the young women, yet in dancing they made use of so many wanton airs, and threw such significant looks towards me, that I was often put to the blush, and obliged to retire to the other side of the room.'

As a regular guest at Lady Anne's balls and dinners, he had ample opportunity to observe Cape society.[4] The majority of British officers and government officials had come to the Cape without their wives, and a number formed liaisons with married Dutch ladies, apparently with the connivance of their husbands, 'who generally walked out when the admirer entered the house'. According to Abu Talib, these families became 'more affluent than when under their own government' as a result of the costly presents that the Englishmen gave their mistresses.

Despite her kindness, some people found Lady Anne's frankness, teasing ways and insatiable curiosity more than a little irritating, and her guest had to submit to a probing inquiry into 'the manners of Industan women and the nature of domestic life there'. She summarised these interesting particulars in her diary, filling several pages in the process.

While Lady Anne's patronage gave Abu Talib *entrée* into colonial society, his Muslim faith enabled him to cross the social and racial divide and mingle with the ex-slaves and Asian immigrants who formed the local free black community. Disillusioned by the conduct of his unscrupulous white landlord, he hired lodgings in a Muslim household and was treated with the greatest attention and kindness. He wrote: 'Among them I met with many pious good Mussulmans, several of whom possessed considerable property. I had the pleasure of forming an acquaintance here with Shaikh Abdulla, the son of Abd al Aziz, a native of Mecca, who, having come on some commercial adventure, married the daughter of one of the Malays, and settled there. He was very civil, introduced me to all his friends, and anticipated all my wishes.'

He had a poor opinion of Cape slave-owners, describing them as repressive and mean:

> If a slave understands any trade, they permit him to work for other people, but oblige him to pay from one to four [Rix]dollars a day, according to his abilities, for such indulgence. The daughters of these slaves who are handsome they keep for their own use, but the ugly ones are either sold, or obliged to work with their fathers. Should a slave perchance save sufficient money to purchase his freedom, they cause him to pay a great price for it, and throw many other obstacles in his way.
>
> I saw a tailor, who was married, and had four children; he was then forty years of age, and had, by great industry and economy, purchased the freedom of himself and his wife; but the children still continued as slaves. One of them, a fine youth, was sold to another master, and carried away to some distant land: the eldest girl was in the service of her master; and the two youngest were suffered to remain with their parents until they should gain sufficient strength to be employed.

Female slaves who made the beds and kept the rooms in order in the town's many lodging houses sometimes obtained money in return for sexual favours. An English officer who had been one of Abu Talib's travelling companions 'formed an attachment to one of the females in the house', but the girl was severely punished when their liaison was discovered, and was 'compelled to pay to her oppressive master all the money the captain had given her ...'

Abu Talib attended Lady Anne's weekly entertainments until his departure in September 1799. When he left, she sent letters to Britain recommending him to the attention of some of her 'best and highest friends'. Thanks partly to this generous impulse, he was welcomed in London as 'The Persian Prince'.

One

Tangled relationships

IN 1658, SIX YEARS after the establishment of Van Riebeeck's refreshment station at the Cape, two shiploads of west African slaves were landed at Table Bay. During the next century and a half, approximately 63 000 despairing captives were imported from the east coast of Africa, Madagascar, Mauritius, Ceylon, India, the Malay Peninsula and the islands that make up modern Indonesia. Finally, in 1838, some 36 000 ex-slaves were released from a four-year apprenticeship, given their freedom, and allowed to take charge of their own poverty.

After the first small shipments, no slaves were imported from places lying to the west of Mozambique, which means that the descendants of South African slaves have different roots to their counterparts in North America and the Caribbean, most of whose ancestors came from the western hinterland of Africa. New cargoes of Indian Ocean slaves continued to arrive erratically until 1807, after which Cape-born slaves (also known as creoles) formed the majority of the slave population. Most slave owners preferred creoles to foreign imports and were prepared to pay a premium for them.

Slavery was introduced to the Cape in direct response to an insatiable need for labour on the part of the Dutch East India Company (*Verenigde Oost-Indische Compagnie*, hereafter VOC). Commander van Riebeeck and his successors were forbidden to enslave local Khoi, San or black people, and although many free-born South Africans were later dispossessed of their ancestral land and reduced to the status of poverty-stricken agricultural labourers, they were technically not slaves.

During the VOC period (1652 to 1795), slavery was characterised by strange contradictions. On one hand, slaves were routinely subjected to cruel treatment and inhumane punishments, including torture, being impaled alive, and hanging, drawing and quartering. On the other hand, a surprising number of slaves were manumitted and baptised, prior to marrying into the free burgher population. Unlike concubinage, marriage conferred lasting social advantages on women of colour and their children. Extra-marital sex was widespread in Cape Town, where there was a floating

population of unattached males, and the Slave Lodge doubled as the port's principal brothel – with the connivance of the authorities.

Contrary to popular apartheid mythology, very few of the whites who lived at the Cape in the eighteenth century wore powdered wigs or silk gowns, and still fewer received invitations to pretentious functions at the Castle. Numerous impoverished, ill-educated men came to the Cape from northern Europe to serve as soldiers or manual workers for the mighty VOC. Most were intent on obtaining burgher papers and acquiring the means to start a business – with the help of a suitably hard-working spouse. One successful shopkeeper and property owner began his career collecting glass bottles from ships in Bay and selling them to farmers. Others were capable journeymen who prospered at their trades.

Marriage partners were something of a problem – there was a shortage of white women at the Cape, and burghers' daughters tended to marry up the social scale. Many immigrants formed liaisons with slaves that developed into lasting attachments and were legitimised by the rites of

3. Using primitive methods, slaves gave substance to a remarkable vernacular architecture. Having first dug a convenient pit, they kneaded water into the exposed clay with their feet. The resulting mixture, often bound with straw or other vegetable matter, was used to build thick, slightly tapering walls and low gables which were carefully plastered. Bricks were also used, but they were expensive to transport and the quality of the local product was often inferior. Drawing by Lady Anne Barnard, c. *1798.*

manumission, baptism and marriage. About 1 000 slave and Khoi brides married colonists during the VOC period and their children were generally assimilated into the white population. The practice declined as more free women became available in the late eighteenth century. Men who were unwilling or unable to marry occasionally freed and baptised the children they procreated with their slave concubines. Today, these tangled relationships – previously denied or ignored – are receiving considerable attention from historians and interest groups intent on revising the one-dimensional social history of the past. The Dutch custom whereby married women retained their maiden names after marriage was in vogue at the Cape until about the middle of the nineteenth century, and this has made it easier to identify the slave women who became Christian wives.

Johann Philipp Reimers, a German from Fishbeck, was employed by the VOC Company as a house-carpenter in 1747, and was on loan, presumably to a well-to-do burgher, from 1749 to 1753. He was released from Company service the following year and died in 1770. His heir was his illegitimate son Jan Fredrik, whose mother was the free woman of colour Agnite of the Cape. She later married another German, Johann Friedrich Israel, a farm-hand who came to the Cape as a soldier in 1737. Johann and Agnite had five children before her death in 1773.

Reimers also had an extra-marital liaison with Christina Susanna of the Cape, a relatively prosperous ex-slave, by whom he had a daughter, baptised in April 1748, who seems to have died young. He married Christina in March 1754, but she died a year later, bequeathing him her house in Burg Street, acquired in 1753.[5] The property consisted of four rooms, a loft and a carpenter's workshop, and was valued at 8 500 Rixdollars. The couple also owned two imported slaves, August of Malabar and Januarij of Bengal, who presumably assisted Reimers in his workshop and slept there.

While she was still a slave, Christina Susanna had given birth to two illegitimate children, Louisa Smith (father unidentified) and Lodewyk Frickel by the German immigrant, Johannes Frickel. In 1749 she applied to manumit these children, and they were baptised in July of that year. She must have been a remarkable woman to have acquired the means both to buy their freedom and obtain a desirable urban property.

Christina Susanna's former mistress was Christina Bergh, widow of the Swedish immigrant Matthijs Bergstedt. Christina Bergh was herself the granddaughter of a slave. She was the eldest daughter of the Swede Olaf Bergh and his wife Anna de Koning, daughter of Angela of Bengal. Although Christina Susanna's manumission record has not been found, Christina Bergh and her husband are known to have freed at least three slaves.

Louisa Smith married soon after Reimers legalised his relationship with her mother. In 1755 she became the wife of Johannes Willem Jansen, sixth child of Jan Jansz of Ceylon and Rosetta of Bengal, a free black couple who had married in November 1737 after Jan purchased Rosetta's freedom. Unfortunately for Louisa, her spouse soon died. Her next husband was a German, Heinrich Adolph Schröder. He arrived as a soldier in 1746 and later worked as a door-keeper at the hospital (situated across the road from the Slave Lodge). He obtained burgher rights in 1758, and later that year he married the widowed Louisa. The couple had six children before he died in 1771. Schröder had an older illegitimate son – the result of a liaison with a slave named Annetta. In 1757, while he was still employed by the Company, Schröder applied to manumit his little slave boy, named Adolph of the Cape, thus formally adopting him. Louisa's third and final marriage was to another German, Michael Gerens, a sailor who arrived in 1766 and applied for burgher rights in 1771. He subsequently set up as a shoemaker. Her eldest son, Jan Hendrik Schröder, married twice and had 14 children, many of whom married into well-known Cape families.

Although most German immigrants were law-abiding and responsible citizens, there were some flamboyant characters among them. Joachim

Kannemeyer, a sword-cutler, arrived in 1747 and became foreman of the armoury in 1751. He married a Dutch wife, Johanna Adriana Arends of the Hague, but divorced her in 1752 after the birth of his daughter Maria Johanna. Before his marriage he had fathered a son and two daughters by a free black woman, Christina Vogel, and after his divorce he sired a further nine children by Magdelena of the Cape.

Despite these promising signs, prosperity bred prejudice, and racial intolerance stiffened during the latter part of the eighteenth century. Most of the hard physical work was done by slaves and indigenous labourers, and some colonists grew increasingly lazy and self-satisfied, content to direct underlings rather than lead by example. Slave ownership conferred status, and working for others was considered demeaning. A young man who possessed a wagon, a horse, a gun and a few head of stock would push into the interior and acquire a 'loan-place' for a small annual rental. When his fortunes improved he would invest in slaves – commodities that could be readily mortgaged, transferred, sold or bequeathed. Slaves could cohabit but not marry, and the children conceived by a female slave became her owner's property from the moment they were born – even if he or some other white man was their natural father. This pattern survived the terminal decline of the VOC and three changes of administration between 1795 and 1806.

The increasingly vociferous anti-slavery lobby in Europe was scarcely heard at the Cape. The tempo of slave imports increased during the First British Occupation, much to the satisfaction of local owners, and the abolition of the oceanic slave trade in the British Empire in 1807 was greeted with disbelief and dismay. Momentous as this step was, it meant little to those already in bondage, and existing slaves and their offspring were marketed locally until 1834. Prices fluctuated widely during this period, peaking in the 1820s with negative consequences for slaves and owners alike.

The sense of hopeless alienation (sometimes termed 'social death') experienced by many slaves was arguably less agonising in Cape Town than in the country districts. Rural slaves led hard, monotonous, circumscribed lives and suffered the worst abuse. Urban slaves had far more mobility and in the 1820s about 2 000 were either hired out to other employers or were allowed to live out and ply their trades for their own account, provided they paid their owners a regular monthly fee known as *koeliegeld*. They could use their surplus earnings to buy their freedom or that of their wives and children. They were generally better informed and more sophisticated than slaves who lived in isolation on the farms, and they shared a vibrant underclass culture with members of the small but highly visible free black community. However, urban slavery declined during the 27 years following the abolition of the international slave trade, and almost 3 000 slaves were sold up-country to alleviate the chronic shortage of agricultural and domestic labour. To be transferred to strangers who lived in another district was a painful and demoralising experience for any slave. Familiar landmarks vanished as the wagon crossed the first range of mountains, and precious bonds of kinship were often severed for life.

Free blacks occupied an intermediate position between privileged white burghers and powerless slaves. They lived in rented accommodation in the poorer streets and alleys of Cape Town. The men worked as masons, painters, carpenters, blacksmiths, tallow chandlers, basket makers, tailors, cobblers, fishermen, boatmen, porters, hawkers and small retailers, while the women were generally washerwomen or seamstresses. Slaves had similar skills, and they often worked together. They were all exiles or the descendants of exiles, they understood a common Malayo-Portuguese *lingua franca*, and they shared a similar world view. They were linked by bonds of kinship and affection, and they spent their free time in each other's company. Men enjoyed illegal games of chance – cards, gambling and cock fighting – and mingled with soldiers and sailors in taverns and *smokkelhuise* (shebeens), where they caroused and drank cheap liquor. Many were musically gifted and could play a variety of instruments by ear. They particularly enjoyed picnics and outings. According Samuel Hudson, slaves tried to accumulate 'decent apparel' to sport on a Sunday. 'I have seen them with their wives and children very well attired, taking their walks or dancing to their rude music ... or joining their Rixdollars for the hire of a wagon and spend the afternoon at some of the dancing houses in the country.' The women loved to dance, and those who attended 'rainbow balls' – mixed assemblies where the lower classes could enjoy themselves – were sometimes as smart and graceful as their mistresses.

Ignored by the local Dutch Reformed clergy, many adopted the Muslim faith and found it gave them significant spiritual and social consolation. But although shared experiences fostered solidarity, poverty prevented the development of any real underclass stability. Many free black families moved from one hired room or shared cellar to another with distressing regularity. It was difficult to raise healthy families under such circumstances and child mortality was high, especially during epidemics.

Readers may find it difficult to picture a society where men, women and children were bought, mortgaged, sold, transferred, bequeathed, or rented out as commodities. In the 1820s a Cape Town newspaper called the *South African Chronicle and Mercantile Advertiser* carried English and Dutch advertisements for items as diverse as ponies, properties, casks of butter, flannel shirts, tallow candles, hymn books – and slaves. The columns for 1825 and 1826 provide a taste of what it was like to be a human chattel.[6]

> 'Mrs Sleigh informs the public that among her slaves who are to be sold, she can recommend to any genteel English or Dutch family, two African female slaves: one named Martha (good tempered), aged 23, who is a capital nurse[maid], milliner, lady's maid, pleats and irons well, and can do housework in general; the other, named Lea (good tempered, and perfectly white), who is a wet nurse, with three fine children, the eldest seven years old. She is also a capital

nurse[maid], lady's maid, milliner, laundress, and can do house work in general; both are cooks. They have excellent characters, and having served Mrs Sleigh attentively and obediently, it is hoped they may be disposed of to a genteel and kind family.'

'For private sale, some clever baker boys; also a clever gardener and coachman – not parted with on account of any fault, but because their master has no further employment for them.'

'Ran away, about 14 days ago, an old Malay slave named April, about sixty years of age, and turns his large toes inwards. Whoever apprehends said slave, and will lodge him in the Tronk, shall receive 15 Rixdollars reward. Those harbouring him will be prosecuted.'

'Wanted to hire, a slave girl of good character, who understands plain needlework and getting up linen.'

'Ran away, from the house No 58, Loop-street, a male slave, dressed in a blue kersey jacket, nankeen trowsers, and had a red hand-kerchief round his head. It is supposed he may have gone to the country with a false pass, which he has done twice before.'

'To let, a healthy wet nurse. Apply to JJ Steytler, Green Point.'

'For sale, a clever housemaid, with her three male children, the eldest of whom [is] about 15, one 11, the other 9 years old. The first has been employed for twelve months as a mason.'

'Sale by the Sequestrator to this Government ... the slaves July, Fytje of Mosambique, Sabina, Rosina, Fytje, Delia, Rachel, and Fortuin of the Cape ... Said slaves, comprising one family, will first be put up separately, and afterwards as one lot, when in the event of their yielding more at the separate bidding, the persons making that offer will become the purchasers.'

'Jek of Mosambique, aged about 27 years, is for sale, owing to his disobedience: a farmer will have the preference.'

'For sale, the slave maid Regina of the Cape ... She is an excellent washer, ironer, cook, and housemaid, and would be found very useful on a farm. The purchase money may remain 3 years on interest if required.'

'A Mosambique slave boy, about 30 years of age, well worthy of the attention of any gentleman requiring a very fine wholesome young man, in perfect good health, will be sold at Mr Reeve's Commission Sales ... He is a plain cook and a house servant, and a complete master of all agricultural business.'

Prior to the opening of the first savings bank at the Cape in 1837, people with modest amounts of capital often lived off their investment in human bondage. Elderly people and widows would hire slaves out to other people by the month and use the money to buy the necessities of life. Artisans and wet nurses commanded good wages and were always in demand, but girls of 14 were sent out to care for children and do plain needlework, and slave children were farmed out to save their owners the expense of maintaining them. The system was fraught with problems. Slaves who were sick or injured were unable to work, and owners were at risk of penury if they died. Others absconded for weeks at a time and sometimes never returned. Disobedient slaves were difficult to place, and owners sustained financial losses if they were imprisoned for serious crimes.

In August 1830, two female slaves, Rachel and Lea of the Cape, and a free black woman named Leentje were charged with stealing numerous articles from the Longmarket Street home of Leentje's employer, Robert Shearer, a pub keeper. The missing items included jewellery, a toothpick, twelve dozen mother-of-pearl buttons, silk stockings, a smelling bottle, tortoise shell combs, three cheese plates, a pair of trousers and two yards of lace. Rachel was found guilty of theft and of passing stolen goods to the others. She was sentenced to be transported from the Colony for seven years to such place as the governor should direct, pending which she was to be imprisoned and kept at government labour. Lea and Leentje were each sentenced to two years in the female prison known as the House of Correction.[7]

Within days Sir Lowry Cole received memorials from two sisters begging him to commute the sentences. Anna van Eyssen (1793 to 1869), widow of the late Johan Stadler, explained that the earnings of Rachel formed the chief part of her income, and her spinster sister Aletta van Eyssen (1808 to 1867) stated that she had no other means of support than the earnings of Lea, and that if the sentence were to be enforced she would not know 'whereof to find clothes and other necessaries of life.'[8]

The sisters had family connections, so they had somewhere to turn when their petitions were rejected, but it was no doubt mortifying to assume the humble status of poor relations. Anna went to stay with her father-in-law at the farm Groote Post, and Aletta moved in with the Melcks at the Berg River. In December 1830 they forwarded a joint petition to the governor that throws some additional light on their circumstances. Anna (37) claimed to be a very poor widow with two dependent children, one of whom had been ill for about a year without her mother being able to afford medical treatment for her. The slave Rachel brought in the paltry sum of eight Rixdollars a month, on which the widow contrived to clothe herself and her children. Now that she was deprived of that income, she was embarrassed and in the greatest distress. Both Rachel and Lea had always behaved with propriety and honesty until they were led astray, and Rachel had two little children, also slaves, whom Anna was obliged to maintain while their mother was in prison. Aletta (22) was a poor orphan who had no other means of subsistence than the income that Lea brought her and the generosity of the Melcks. The sisters begged His Excellency to return their slaves to their service, to enable them to find a manner of living.[9]

Cole relented, and their petition is endorsed: 'Instructions given that Rachel and Lea be restored to their owners, the former after serving 12 and the latter 6 months of their sentences.' No one thought to tell Rachel of her reprieve, and in March 1831 she forwarded her own petition from Robben Island, begging not to be sent to New South Wales on account of her poor health, needy children and the 'aged' mistress who depended on her for an income. Fortunately the governor remembered her case, and she was released after serving her shortened sentence.[10]

Risky as it was, the practice of hiring out slaves was so firmly entrenched that talk of emancipation threw many owners into a panic. They had reason to be nervous: the compensation they eventually received was less than they expected, and they had to arrange for agents to collect it in London, resulting in long delays and extra expense. The Van Eyssen sisters managed to preserve some of their capital, but they did not prosper; both died in the late 1860s, leaving small estates. Anna's daughters inherited a secure nest egg of £42.[11] Aletta had chosen to invest in livestock – she kept eight oxen and fourteen cows and calves on the Melck's farm, hiring grazing and supplying the herdsman with tobacco each month. These animals were valued at just under £49.[12]

Two

The urban scene

ALMOST 16 500 PEOPLE LIVED permanently in Cape Town in 1806, of whom 9 367 were slaves and 6 428 were free people – both white and black. Only 626 inhabitants were of Khoi descent, and there were no Xhosa people at all. These figures exclude members of the civil service, soldiers of the garrison (numbering as many as 4 000 on some occasions) and transient sailors and ships' passengers. Many townsfolk offered lodging and services to visitors, including the British officers and civilian families who came to the Cape from India to recover their health, together with their ayahs and well-dressed Indian servants. Their visits often lasted for six or nine months, and the leading medical men of the day were said to make a very comfortable living.

What was Cape Town like during the last decades of slavery? It was a seaward-looking town, inhabited by a colourful and diverse population, situated on one of the world's great trans-oceanic routes. Viewed from the deck of a sailing ship tossing at anchor in Table Bay, it appeared as a white-washed huddle of buildings surrounded by about fifty 'garden estates' – market gardens belonging to some of the old Cape families. Closer inspection revealed that the densely populated lanes and alleys near Rogge Bay and behind the Castle had already become slums, while squatting, often believed to be a twentieth century phenomenon, took place on the fringes of the town. Numerous tap-houses and canteens catered for the floating population of single men at the lower end of the social scale, and gambling, brawling, prostitution and petty theft were rife. Other areas, particularly the upper end of Dorp Street, where the more settled and prosperous Muslim families lived, seemed more akin to Asia than Africa.

The dung-strewn streets were kept in some sort of order by prisoners under the supervision of the superintendent of police, Baron Charles de Lorentz. Residents were expected to keep the areas in front of their houses well swept and wholesome, but many didn't bother. Waste disposal was rudimentary, particularly in the poorer quarters. The dumping of offensive matter was supposed to take place in the vicinity of Green Point, but scraps and offal from the fish market and the slaughterhouses at the Shambles, both situated near the foot of the Heerengracht, were simply tossed into the sea. Whale boats were drawn up on the beach at the foot of Bree Street, and the carcass of many a beast harpooned by a skilful whaler named Edries added to the pervading stench.[13] Wild animals were still kept in a kind of zoo at the top of the Gardens, and there was a more extensive menagerie owned by Mr Villet at Green Point. Although epidemics were common, mortality was kept in check by the climate. The winter rains flushed out the canals and foetid *steegs*, and the relentless summer wind known as the south-easter blew both rubbish and miasmas out to sea.

The few substantial buildings dating from the VOC period included the Castle, the Great Barracks, Government House, the Groote Kerk, the Lutheran Church, the Town House on Greenmarket Square and the government offices (previously the Slave Lodge). British architecture had not made much impact on the Dutch character of the town, and the only structures of note were a theatre (now St Stephen's Church on Riebeek Square), the Commercial Exchange on the Parade, and St Andrew's Scottish Church in Somerset Road. St George's Church (later the Anglican Cathedral) was not completed until 1834, and the English community gathered for worship in the Dutch Reformed Church, led by the Revd. Hough. There was no resident bishop, and the arrival of one on his way to or from India was looked forward to with eager anticipation, especially by candidates who were anxiously awaiting confirmation.

The Grand Parade was just one block away from the badly polluted shoreline. It was considerably larger in those days, stretching from the Castle to the Heerengracht (now Adderley Street) and from Keizersgracht (now Darling Street) to Stand Street, where the infamous Town Prison (generally known as the Tronk) abutted the Customs House. It was bounded by a low wall and a dirty ditch and surrounded on three sides by a double row of wind-lashed pine trees. The first building to encroach on the Parade was the Commercial Exchange, which was regarded as one of the ornaments of the town when it opened in 1821. Leading merchants patronised its 'great room', and the local dance-loving community attended balls and masquerades in the central hall. The public library was housed in the north wing, and the south wing served as a warehouse for merchandise that was auctioned in the open air several times a week. These lively and interesting sales attracted good crowds, including many who came for the free entertainment.

Fresh produce was sold at the early morning market, which had been moved to a site just beyond the Castle in 1819 to prevent congestion, but the Parade was the main hub of trade. Commodities from all nations were on offer, including manufactured goods and luxury articles from Britain, loaf sugar, rice, coffee and spice from the Dutch dominions and America, matches and daintily carved toys from Germany, and 'skilfully

joined fur rugs' (karosses) from the interior.[14] There were also endless varieties of imported cloth, including beaverteens, nankinets, cantoons and the ever-popular muslins. Ships from the east brought China soy in two gallon jars, preserved and dried ginger, citron, oranges, dates, lichees and tamarinds. Less common items advertised in February 1834 included Kentish hops, isinglass, brown stout, superior window glass, sperm candles and 'a smart, fashionable well-conditioned chariot, elegantly painted and emblazoned, the property of a lady'. Most goods were sold to make way for fresh cargoes of Cape agricultural produce, but passing ships sometimes landed freight that had been spoiled by contact with sea water. Some speculators made a good living buying damaged goods and abandoned articles and selling them at a profit. Horses and livestock were also auctioned on the Parade, and from time to time 'curiosities' (usually rare mammals or freaks) were put on display for a small fee.

The town's economy was dominated by a merchant elite – a small coterie of Britons who had trading partners in London and India – and

4. A slave sweeps the stoep in front of Mrs Barker's retail shop located in a convenient room in her house on the corner of Burg and Castle Streets. Most town houses boasted projecting stoeps which narrowed the streets and forced pedestrians to walk through dust and mud. Sketch by Sir Charles D'Oyly, dated 14.4.1832.

there was considerable excitement when they received their seasonal supplies. The leading firms would circulate notices to the local shopkeepers stating that their merchandise would be open for inspection at a certain hour, and when the doors opened there was a rush and scramble for the first pick.[15] Apart from basic necessities and foodstuffs, almost everything needed to support a comfortable life was imported. Although many townsfolk made their living from buying and selling, there were few shops in the modern sense of the word, and random stocks of goods were sold from the front rooms of private houses. Times were slowly changing, however, and in 1834 George Greig opened a new store on the corner of the Heerengracht and Strand Street which offered an eclectic choice of furniture, fabric, soap, cutlery, parasols, mourning pins, peppermint lozenges, and very fine ladies' full hose (stockings).

The affluent Dutch families employed numerous slaves and servants and enjoyed a good deal of leisure. According to one anonymous writer, 'you might as soon have expected to be served by the dead, as to have entered a shop between the hours of noon and 3 p.m. with the idea of being attended to. Their shops were left in charge of trustworthy slaves, and the invariable reply to a would-be customer was: *"Mijnheer slaap"* or *"Juffrouw slaap"*.'[16] After taking a siesta, families gathered on the high stoeps at the front of their town houses to take tea and preserves, waited on by their slaves. Parties and entertainments were popular, and the slave orchestras assembled by Mr Smuts and Mr van Breda were always in demand. Many of the players were men who had been imported from Mozambique as agricultural labourers, but their astonishing musical proficiency raised their status, and they probably enjoyed some of the minor privileges afforded to indoor servants.

The town's culturally diverse inhabitants were by no means as gracious and tolerant as some writers have led us to believe. Differences in class, wealth, race and religion bred animosities that were liable to flare in a moment. The Parade drew lively and ill-mannered crowds on some occasions, as the shoemaker Joseph Tindall (1807 to 1861) testified in his memoirs.[17] Tindall, a fiery Wesleyan Methodist lay preacher, arrived at the Cape in 1836, together with his wife and child, consumed by a deep desire to save souls in Africa. Finding Methodism 'at a low ebb' in the city, he held evening prayer meetings in his home, sat up all night composing lengthy sermons, and spent his Sundays visiting the back streets and preaching on the Parade. These pious endeavours sparked 'awful scenes' and taunts and orders to be gone.

Slaves had been largely excluded from Christian worship, and some whites were hostile to attempts to convert them. Tindall met with violent and vociferous opposition when slave apprentices and free blacks attended his first Sunday afternoon meeting on the Parade. He wrote: 'We had a large congregation of coloured people, Malays, soldiers, respectable tradesmen and hundreds of pleasure-takers, who joined the congregation for a shorter or longer period, (but) our peace was disturbed by mocking, sneering and shouting ... This roused several of our members who came forward to keep order and to defend us openly.' Tindall advised his supporters to disregard the disturbances and offer no resistance, but instead to reprove and exhort their enemies as the holy spirit moved them. Although he and his party suffered 'damaged clothes and severe blows with stones', he was not discouraged.

Agitators went about the town urging the public to assemble and 'drive such nuisances as lay preaching from their favourite fashionable Sabbath walk'. They sang, shouted and threatened, until preaching became impossible and escape seemed prudent. Tindall walked boldly through the hostile crowd and was allowed to pass unmolested, but his less confident companions were mobbed for another half an hour. The ringleaders later asserted that they were not against ordained ministers preaching on the Parade, but they objected to laymen. However, when the Revd. TL Hodgson and other leading Wesleyans tried to hold a service there, they were given the same reception. According to Tindall, 'Threats, stones and blows were abundant. Myself and a few others were in danger of being forced into a wide deep ditch. A fine man of colour, who had [allowed] his zeal to outrun his discretion, struck one of the disturbers. Many voices then cried "Bring him out and kill him." However, he managed to creep away and so escaped their wrath.' Meanwhile, Revd. Hodgson stood near a tree looking extremely anxious. 'His voice was drowned by the noise, and he thought it time to withdraw – which he did, but not without being pelted.'

Tindall was eventually forced to preach beyond the Parade boundaries. He continued to hold meetings, heedless of provocation, until he left Cape Town to minister to the Nama people at Warmbad in July 1839.

Three

Household chores

ALTHOUGH THE AVERAGE CAPE slave holder owned less than six slaves, some affluent families employed a small army of gardeners, carriers, grooms, coachmen, cooks, housemaids, nursery maids, wet nurses and laundry maids to see to their needs. Why so many? Part of the answer lies in the fact that there were none of the labour-saving devices or municipal services that we take for granted today. Two of the greatest necessities of life – water and wood – had to be collected daily, and food could only be preserved by tedious processes like salting, pickling and drying.

Laundry was particularly labour-intensive, and the practice of sending linen out to be washed rather than drawing on scanty domestic water supplies originated during the first days of settlement and lasted long after the gradual introduction of piped water and drainage in the nineteenth century. Although initially an occupation for slaves, there were more than a hundred free black laundresses active in Cape Town by 1820, and the unsupervised mingling of slave and free women helped to consolidate a common underclass culture.

The Platteklip Stream in the upper Table Valley seems to have become a recognised washing place by about 1700. The route to the washing pools led from the top of what is now Upper Buitenkant in Vredehoek along an attractive lane known as the 'slave walk'. It passed the gracious homesteads of Rheezicht and Nooitgedacht (now St Cyprian's School) and then followed the course of the Capel Sluit on the boundary of the historic Oranjezicht estate. The path was shaded in summer, and the banks of the stream were covered with arums in winter.

Washerwomen needed to be fit and strong. Soap was scarce and it was the custom to beat the dirt out of the clothes while standing up to their knees in cold water. Some clients, startled by the rapid deterioration of their shirts and linen, accused the women of heavy-handedness, and a recent archaeological dig in the bed of the Platteklip stream has turned up thousands of buttons, buckles and pins.[18] The weather played a large part in their lives, and cycles of drought, wind and rain seriously affected their productivity, but on fine days the lower slopes of Devil's Peak and Table Mountain were decked with linen bleaching in the sun. The dry garments were folded and returned to their clients in bundles carried on their heads. Copper smoothing irons filled with live embers were used for ironing – a tedious task requiring particular skill.

Male slaves who were employed to collect firewood also escaped the reproving gaze of their owners, but their task was much harder. Periodic fires and decades of indiscriminate hewing had reduced the Cape Peninsula's indigenous forests to a few small patches hidden in rugged kloofs on Table Mountain. In 1811, the Scottish soldier James Ewart wrote:

> There is little or no wood near Cape Town, if I except the brushwood which grows in the clefts of the mountains, and in small clumps in the sandy vleis. Several plantations of firs and oaks have lately been tried along the south side of the Table which seem to thrive well ... Those who have the severest task to perform are the slaves who are sent to the country for firewood, for a couple of bundles of which they have often to go a distance of ten or twelve miles, carrying them home on the ends of a piece of bamboo laid across their shoulders, and it is astonishing with what celerity they move with a load which I have found difficult to raise from the ground.[19]

When fresh ground was cultivated, slaves with billhooks would clear it of heath and scrub and the brushwood would usually be sent to town in wagons and sold to bakers. The demand for firewood was so insatiable that escaped slaves hiding on Table Mountain were said to eke out a precarious existence working as illegal woodcutters. Their bundles were collected by slaves who were allowed to work on their own account and pay *koeliegeld*. They would leave small caches of food and tobacco for the runaways.

Some piped water was available in Cape Town during the early British period, but most households drew domestic supplies from wells and widely dispersed public fountains. During the 1820s numerous petitions were forwarded to the governor requesting new fountains on the grounds that slaves or servants had to walk up to 500 meters to fetch buckets of water. Mr Skirrow, the Waterworks Superintendent, had a limited budget and was frequently unsympathetic, but the total eventually reached 63, mainly in the affluent areas. Slaves mingled freely at public fountains and were able to meet friends, exchange gossip and engage in barter.

Sanitation was a tremendous problem in the built-up areas. In 1799 the Persian visitor Abu Talib ibn Muhammad Khan commented scathingly on local arrangements, particularly 'the filthiness and stench of the privies, which they take no pains to keep clean. Neither have they any [public] baths, either hot or cold, in the town; ablution is quite unknown to the inhabitants.'[20] Human waste was either channelled into cesspits or emptied into the household privy tub, an evil-smelling wooden container that

had to be drained at regular intervals. The dumping of effluent in drains or ditches within the town limits was strictly forbidden, but this was common practice in the worst of the slums, where few officials dared to venture. Periodically – usually after an epidemic – convicts were deployed to remove the accumulated muck.

The designated place for emptying privy tubs was the beach between the Amsterdam Battery (near the foot of present-day Ebenezer Road) and the Chavonnes Battery (near the Clocktower precinct at the Victoria and Alfred Waterfront). Land reclamation and harbour construction during the last 150 years have completely altered the original coastline, but the practice of disposing of sewage and other waste in the sea off the Atlantic coast continues.

One morning in April 1831 the slaves Sava (alias Sabang of Macoa) and Urbanus of Ceylon, both about 50 years old, left the Plein Street house of their mistress, Helena Maria, widow of Advocate Ryk le Sueur, and set off in tandem for the beach with the privy tub suspended by means of a rope

5. The Heerengracht in 1832, with town houses and business premises on the right and the Groote Kerk and Parade – lined by a polluted canal and an avenue of trees – on the left. There is a Muslim fish vendor in the foreground, and most of the pedestrians appear to be slaves. Sketch by Sir Charles D'Oyly, dated 20.4.1832.

from a pole carried on their shoulders. Their route took them through the heart of the main residential and commercial district to the crowded lanes near Rogge Bay, past the original Somerset Hospital and down to what must have been a seriously polluted beach. They had made the trip hundreds, if not thousands, of times before, but on that particular day the rope attached to the tub slipped, and they had the ill luck to spill the waste in front of a house in the Heerengracht occupied by William Billingsley, an English merchant and shipping agent. They were arrested by a policeman who accused them of deliberately dumping their load, taken into custody, brought before the judge of police, and sentenced to fines of twenty shillings each or, in default of payment, imprisonment for four days.[21]

The widow Le Sueur, then 60 years old, was a member of one of the Cape's foremost Dutch families and the mother of twelve children. Her household included eight slaves – five adults and three children.[22] She was convinced that Sava and Urbanus were innocent, and begged the governor to graciously remit the fines, protesting that 'far from shewing any marks of guilt by avoiding detection, [they] were endeavouring to take up the filth when they were suddenly apprehended …'[23]

She testified that they both bore very good characters, particularly Sava, 'who for the last 30 years has led an irreproachable life and been employed in carrying away the filth of his mistress' house without giving cause for complaint,' and pointed out that it was unlikely that they would have gone as far as Mr Billingsley's house to empty a tub that they might more easily and conveniently have drained in a ditch close to her house near the Parade. Baron de Lorentz, the sometimes eccentric judge of police, was unmoved, and told the governor that Mrs le Sueur's version of the mishap had not come to light in court. Sir Lowry Cole chose not to exercise his discretion, and her memorial is endorsed: 'Cannot be complied with.'

Four

Slave sympathisers

ALTHOUGH THE EARLY EUROPEAN missionaries are often denounced for bolstering colonial dispossession, their records and reports are valuable historical documents that highlight social conditions during the first half of the nineteenth century. Whatever their faults – and cultural insensitivity was certainly one – they were generally far more sympathetic than the majority of colonists to the plight of the underclasses.

The London Missionary Society (LMS) commenced work in South Africa in 1799, and within a decade farmers were accusing it of bias in favour of the Khoikhoi. The Society's directors in London were aware of these and other tensions, and in 1812 they sent one of their colleagues to the Cape to make a thorough inspection of the different missionary settlements.

Revd. John Campbell (1776 to 1840), the youngest son of an Edinburgh greengrocer, had been apprenticed to a goldsmith in his youth, but strong religious convictions led to his ordination in the 1790s. He spent 17 months in South Africa, and was the first missionary traveller to make a long tour of the interior, visiting isolated mission stations as far north as Lattakoo, near present day Kuruman. He undertook a similar gruelling journey seven years later, and his manuscript journals and sketchbooks reflect his fortitude and his diligent, gentle nature.[24]

Campbell arrived in Table Bay on 24 October, 1812 after a difficult four-month passage and was hospitably accommodated by Mr Constant van Nuldt Onkruydt, president of the Burgher Senate. The cool weather travelling season was over, and he was advised to defer his tour until the midsummer heat had abated. Campbell deplored slavery, but he noted that some owners were more indulgent than others. The Onkruydts were benevolent paternalists who treated their adult slaves as if they were adolescents. Their slave children were sent to school and were permitted to play about the room where the family gathered for meals 'with as much freedom, and receive as much attention, as if they were their own children – but alas! they are slaves!' It was in their master's interest to ensure that they were well treated, 'on the same principle on which the farmer takes care of his young foals, because by their death, or disease, he becomes the loser'. Slaves were not permitted to marry, a prohibition that Campbell regarded as an act of great injustice towards them and a heinous sin against God. However, he was pleased to discover that many couples bound themselves to each other as husbands and wives by mutual consent.

While waiting in Cape Town, he visited Mrs Smit's free school for slaves, 'which meets two or three times a week, and contains about 150 people, black and brown, from six to thirty years of age'. The widow Machtelt Smit (1749 to 1821), known to the English as 'Mother Smith', was a remarkable person – the first South African woman to rise to prominence in her own right. At a time when women took no part in public life, she was actively involved in the evangelisation of people of colour in Cape Town, Tulbagh and Bethelsdorp, and she enjoyed the confidence of a number of prominent missionaries, including the redoubtable Dr Johannes Theodorus van der Kemp.[25]

According to Campbell, she sat on an elevated platform in the centre of the meeting house, instructing her slave pupils in reading, leading them in singing, and concluding her lessons with solemn prayers. Her intense piety attracted a small following of like-minded men and women, several of whom assisted at her school. Their zeal was in sharp contrast to prevailing colonial attitudes. According to Samuel Hudson, an English resident writing in 1806, many owners believed that if slaves were taught to read they would be privy to their masters' secrets and cheat them. Elementary education – where it existed – had a strong religious bias and was generally limited to reading, spelling, singing and Christian instruction. Writing, arithmetic and secular subjects – keys to enhanced status and economic advancement – remained the prerogative of the middle classes until the 1850s. Despite the strong emphasis on spiritual instruction, slave baptisms were infrequent, and between 1810 and 1824 there were only 86 in the entire colony.

After a month in Cape Town, Campbell boarded the post wagon one morning, bound for the little village of Stellenbosch, where he planned to spend the summer. The local LMS evangelist and teacher was Mewes Jans Bakker (1764 to 1824), a former Dutch seaman, who had been running a slave school since 1799. The extension of basic education to rural people of colour was a significant initiative at a time when many burgher children grew up in comparative ignorance. Classes were held two or three times a week in an outbuilding behind Bakker's Dorp Street house. The Netherlands Missionary Society sent occasional boxes of free school books – a particular blessing, as 'ABC books' cost one Rixdollar each in Stellenbosch in 1808. According to Bakker, the notion that slaves could be taught to read Dutch texts had caused a stir in the district – some inhabitants declared that it was an impossible task, and suggested that he would be more likely to succeed with a parrot.[26]

Campbell attended a Sabbath service for adult slaves and left this description:

> At half past two o'clock I attended Mr Bakker's slave meeting, which was a very interesting scene. They met in a large room in his house. About 180 were present, the majority of whom were females. The service began by Mrs Bakker reading a chapter of scripture. Mr B. then gave out a psalm, after which Mr Kicherer [a visiting former LMS missionary] addressed them.
>
> Everyone seemed to hang on his lips: one was singularly earnest in listening, which attracted Mr Kicherer's attention so much as to induce him, in the middle of his discourse, to ask him two or three questions about Jesus, which he answered with a pleasing smile ... The slaves sung as well as the people called Christians, which means, in South Africa, white people.

Campbell was impressed when several members of the congregation stayed behind to speak to Kicherer after the service, including one woman who spoke with particular fervour, regardless of all about her.

Later, he inquired about the slave who had answered Kicherer's questions, and was told that he had long been an excellent Christian:

> Formerly his master would not permit him to attend Mr Bakker, and one day assured him he would flog him if he went. The poor slave with Christian gentleness, said in reply, 'I must tell the Lord that.' The saying so wrought upon his master's mind, that he not only permitted him to go, but likewise all the slaves in his house; and yesterday this gentleman and his lady attended the slave meeting themselves. This slave thanks God for bringing him from Mosambique, his native country.

Bakker took Campbell to meet some of his supporters, including a 'person in business', who was married to a former slave whom Bakker had converted twelve years previously. The prosperous couple owned many slaves. Bakker's success may have owed something to his sympathetic nature. Campbell described him as 'a humble, affectionate, gentle, quiet man: he prays much and says little: is little known and little spoken of, except in his immediate circle; but God has greatly owned his labours.'

A few years later another traveller with a penetrating gaze sailed into Table Bay. During the voyage Marten Douwe Teenstra (1795 to 1864), a well-educated young gentleman farmer from Holland, was smitten by a painful form of paralysis that may have been caused by rheumatic fever, and he arrived in a pitiable condition. The sufferer, who was en route to Java, confronted his difficulties courageously and was eventually re-united with his wife and children. In 1830 he published a reliable and detailed account of his four-month involuntary visit to the Cape in 1825.[27]

On arrival, the passengers had to wait for the ship's papers to be examined before they could disembark. Many people of colour rowed out in small boats, bringing baskets of fresh fish, live crayfish and delicious fruit, knowing that these items, so cheap ashore, would initially command high prices. The ship's cook was on hand to prepare the crayfish for immediate consumption. Once the formalities were complete, the fashionably dressed passengers were rowed across to the Castle jetty by these barefoot boatmen, who wore the simple garb of the poor: brown leather breeches, a short jacket and a conical straw hat.

Teenstra arranged to go ashore to seek medical assistance, and his book contains a wryly humorous account of his unceremonious arrival in town. Early next morning he had himself lowered by rope into a small boat and transported to the jetty. There he remained, alone and friendless, until two scantily-clad black men seized his luggage and made off with it, apparently deaf to his protestations. Then two more slaves arrived, grabbed him by the collar and legs, and bore him away at a trot. They dumped him amongst his boxes aboard a waiting wagon and left without a word. He eventually found comfortable accommodation in Burg Street, in the home of a well-connected spinster, Miss Susanna Truter, where he received the most careful attention from her devoted companion, Miss Louisa Pothoff, the granddaughter of Christina of the Cape, a manumitted slave. Teenstra's physician, Dr van Oosterzee, prescribed an alarming course of treatment that included purges, laxatives, *kwikpillen*, opium, and the application of leeches. Not surprisingly, his condition immediately deteriorated, but eventually, thanks to Miss Pothoff's careful nursing, he was able to enjoy short excursions in a carriage put at his disposal by Susanna's nephew, Advocate Truter. As he was still unable to walk, he hired a sturdy slave named Arend to carry him and attend to his needs at a cost of 45 Rixdollars a month.

The next step in his recuperation was a visit to the hot baths at Caledon. Despite his weakness, he enjoyed the journey in an elderly farmer's jolting wagon and took an intelligent interest in his surroundings. The bath-house, which had been completed fourteen years earlier, contained a number of gloomy, ill-furnished rooms with dung-smeared floors. The only other patient died within hours of their arrival, and Arend was so unnerved by the brooding atmosphere that he fled to the village, convinced that the building was haunted. The invalid, left to shift for himself for 36 hours until his predicament was discovered, somehow managed to kill and cook a chicken. The reluctant Arend was fetched back from Caledon by the local field cornet, and another slave was hired to keep him company. Teenstra was dubious about the benefits he derived from bathing, but he eventually grew strong enough to hobble about and ride a quiet horse. He paid visits to nearby farms and arranged wagon excursions to the Moravian mission village at Genadendal and the stalactite caves at Gansbaai. Although he was grateful for the generous hospitality he received, his enlightened views and youthful idealism made him critical of local attitudes towards slaves and free people of colour.

By the time he returned to Cape Town he was well on the road to recovery, and he spent the next few weeks exploring the town and observing local customs. He visited the Tronk, and was appalled by the cruelties he witnessed. Some prisoners, virtually naked, were kept chained like animals, while in the courtyard, tied to a post, a wailing female slave was receiving 39 lashes at the request of her owner. Ten or twelve slaves dressed merely in breeches were undergoing long hours of punishment on the treadmill, watched by a callous, unkempt guard. According to Teenstra, owners were known to send particularly obstinate slaves to the treadmill on six to eight successive days in order to reduce them to a state of helpless exhaustion.

He remarked that many Cape slave-owners *'leeft hier lui en lekker'* (enjoyed a life of indolence and luxury). While in the Overberg, he had seen female slaves serving a gargantuan midday meal to a household of about 20 people – the farmer, his grown-up children and grandchildren and their spouses. Meanwhile, two almost naked male slaves stood near the table keeping the flies away with fans of ostrich feathers. Everything was left to the care of the slaves, and the farmer's beautifully dressed daughters attended to nothing, even having their children suckled by wet nurses.

Slave women were encouraged to procreate, as each new infant added to the master's wealth, and a well-trained young slave would later command a high price. Teenstra met one prosperous woman in Cape Town who told him that she had a large farm on the other side of the mountains where she practiced stock farming and slave breeding. In his opinion, such effortless wealth bred laziness and carelessness, and explained the lamentable lack of industry, economy and discretion he noticed among Cape farmers. Although he found them to be kindly, generous, hospitable, humane and religious, they had become accustomed to their privileged lifestyle and refused to hear any criticism of slavery. Whenever he raised the subject, they accused him of parading his European prejudices, and asserted that the slave-trade was approved by God and the Bible. They declared that slaves were reconciled to their lot, and needed caring masters to feed and clothe them and keep them healthy. Emancipation would bring misery to both masters and slaves, as the latter would refuse to work, and would either starve or take to the mountains and become bandits.

Teenstra believed that owners had become insensible to the injustice they were perpetuating, and cited the recent slave uprising and murders in the Bokkeveld as proof of the deep desire most slaves felt for liberty. In one of only two slave rebellions recorded in South Africa, a small band of disaffected slaves and Khoi farm labourers banded together with the intention of attacking their oppressive masters and marching to Cape Town to claim their freedom. After their capture, they complained of extreme ill-treatment, and medical evidence showed that Galant, their leader, had been excessively punished on numerous occasions. Teenstra later obtained permission to visit the three condemned ringleaders in the Tronk. Galant, who was chained to a block, expressed remorse for his actions, but blamed his former owner for his misfortunes. The prisoners were executed at Worcester soon afterwards and, in a grim warning to other restless slaves, their severed heads were displayed on stakes in the Bokkeveld.

Teenstra also attended the sale of a deceased estate, where 19 slaves and their children were put up for auction. One by one they stepped upon the table to be sold to the highest bidder, gazing round anxiously to see who their new owner would be. Included among the slaves was an old Mozambique woman, her hair white with age, who supported herself on the table with a crutch. She tearfully appealed to the bystanders not to buy her as she was no longer capable of labour. 'Sieur! why do you want to buy me? I can't work any more. This old person can do nothing but keep the fire going in the kitchen and peel potatoes ...' The heirs finally decided to take her back, but her joy soon turned to the direst grief when her thirteen-year old grandson, whom she had reared from infancy after his mother died in childbirth, was sold to a farmer from the eastern frontier, a 40-day journey away. Realising this, the panic-stricken boy jumped from the table crying most pitifully for his foster mother, but he was caught and bound before the distraught old woman's eyes. She could only wring her emaciated hands in an agony of grief as he tried to reach out to her from the wagon that carried him away.

Teenstra, who was powerfully affected by this heartrending scene, denounced the owners as Christians who flouted the teaching of Christ and ignored the common brotherhood of man.

Five

Family ties

THERE ARE HUNDREDS OF thousands of fascinating official documents in the Cape Town Archives Repository in Roeland Street, far too many for one person to read in a lifetime. Among the most poignant are the court records concerning slaves who were punished for crimes of jealousy and passion. Slaves could not marry according to Christian rites prior to 1823, but they were usually allowed to select sexual partners on a casual basis. However, gender ratios were skewed, particularly on the farms, and many male slaves were unable to find concubines, resulting in intense rivalry and high levels of pent-up anger. These tensions led inevitably to promiscuity, rape and other social evils.

Moses of the Cape

One dark evening in April 1797, Moses of the Cape, slave of Christiaan Fick of Stellenbosch, set off to visit his consort, Sabina of the Cape, who belonged to Pieter Gerhardus Wium, one of the heemraden of the village. Moses had his master's permission to be out at night and he carried a lantern, as was required by law. During his journey he met January of Bengal (36), who drew his knife and challenged him with the words: *'Wat seg jij nu?'* (What do you say now?)

Moses was unarmed, but he used his lantern to defend himself, meanwhile calling desperately for help. Despite being stabbed in the chest, he managed to throw his assailant to the ground and wrest the knife from him, wounding his hand in the process. Hearing his shouts, his comrades Fortuyn, September and Carolus rushed to his assistance. They quickly subdued and bound January and delivered him to the village gaol. Moses recovered, but January had harmed a burgher's property and he faced serious charges. He confessed that the attack had been motivated by jealousy because he suspected that his fellow slave Philida had been having carnal relations with Moses. He had previously challenged his rival on this score, saying: *'Jij bent met Philida in de wyngaerd geweest, ik zal jouw krijge!'* (You have been with Philida in the vineyard, I'll catch you!). He claimed that he had intended to hurt and frighten Moses, but not to kill him.[28]

January was scourged, put in irons, and sent to labour on the public works for twelve months. His master had to keep him in chains for another four years, and he was forbidden to appear in public in the village until his sentence had expired.

Felix of Bougies

The shortage of female slaves in the country districts led some slaves to court free Khoi women. The offspring of these unions were technically free, but they could be apprenticed by the farmers on whose farms they were born until they reached the age of 25. In 1798 an elderly slave belonging to Charles Theron, a churchwarden at Roodezand (Tulbagh) was charged with murder. Felix of Bougies, judged to be about 69 years old, had worked for Theron for 34 years. When he was about 40 he began to cohabit with Mitta, Theron's teenage Khoi servant, and during the next 27 years the couple procreated 13 children.

In 1797 Mitta, then aged about 40, went to work for Wynand du Plessis, deacon of the Roodezand church. Having dismissed Felix and wanting nothing more to do with him, she formed a liaison with a slave named Salomon of the Cape. Despite this rebuff, Felix later claimed to have spent the occasional night with her as her husband, although she asserted that he was merely visiting their children. One Sunday in May 1798, Felix called on Mitta and decided to remain overnight in her quarters. Salomon, resenting the intrusion, beat the old man and drove him out, whereupon Felix drew his knife and stabbed his rival so severely in the stomach 'that he in a few minutes afterwards expired'.

Felix and Mitta stood trial together in the Court of Justice.[29] When questioned, he said that he had intended merely to frighten the man who had treated him so badly, but was driven to stab him by grief of heart, because Salomon had first had connection with his daughter, and had afterwards lived 'in fleshly converse' with her mother. Mitta confessed that she had known very well that Salomon had tried to obtain her daughter for his bedfellow, but had let her go because his master disapproved, and engaged himself to Mitta instead. In August 1798 the couple were brought to the usual place of execution in Tulbagh and delivered to the common hangman. Felix was hanged, and his dead body was dragged to another gallows outside the village, 'to be hung up again to remain there until the air and the birds shall have consumed the same'. Having witnessed his execution, Mitta was tied to a post and severely scourged with rods on her bare back, before being sent home.

Henrietta of the Cape

Despite their wider choice of partners, some slave women also succumbed to jealousy. In 1819 Johannes Rabe (1755 to 1821), a farmer in the Hex River valley, purchased an urban slave named Saida (29) on behalf of his daughter and son-in-law, and precipitated a chain of events that culminated in attempted murder. His housemaid, Henrietta of Mauritius (25), was tormented by heartache when her consort Mentor deserted her for the new slave. One Sunday in November, towards noon, Henrietta sent a message asking Saida to keep her company, as she was sick. Saida came as soon as she had dressed her children Bathseba and Salomon, leaving her infant Caatje asleep in her room. The women discussed various matters, including a possible remedy for Henrietta's stomach ache. Henrietta offered her visitor food and oranges, and then suggested a walk to the slaves' gardens, which were situated on a hillside crossed by a deep ditch, some 180 paces from her quarters. Saida was not very impressed with Henrietta's 'beautiful' garden, and she decided to return home in case her baby started crying, which might earn her a beating from her mistress.

On the way back, Saida noticed that Henrietta was carrying a whip, which she claimed to have found at the entrance to the gardens. Saida remarked that the riem would come in handy, as Henrietta's children, who tended the cattle, could use it to secure bundles of reeds and rushes to carry home, but her companion did not reply. Then, as Saida stepped over a little ditch, Henrietta suddenly cried: *'Neen, die zweep is voor jou,'* (No, this whip is for you), and looped the riem over her head from behind. She twisted it so violently that it was only with the greatest difficulty that Saida managed to get her hand over her throat to prevent being strangled. Henrietta let go of the whip, seized her rival by the hair and began beating her head with a large stone. Saida begged to be spared for the sake of her children, but Henrietta knocked her skull against the bank, rendering her temporarily senseless, and pulled her to the ground.

At this point Henrietta's brother November, who had been repairing Saida's bed, came to tell her that her baby was awake. As he intervened, Henrietta cried: *'Broer, broer, laat my bygaan, ik heb haar reeds zooverre door gebracht, laat ik haar nu verder door brengen, ik zal tog wel daar voor myn straf krijgen.'* (Brother, brother, let me alone, I have already got her so far, let me continue, I shall get my punishment for it.) Saida fled, bleeding from eight wounds to the head, and November marched Henrietta off to the farmhouse, from where she was transported to the drostdy at Tulbagh and brought into the hands of justice.[30] Later a shallow hole was discovered a few paces from the ditch, which the prosecutor claimed was a ready-made grave, but Henrietta denied this and said she had merely been preparing a bed in which to plant onions.

Her only defence was to say that she had acted in a passion occasioned by Saida having consented to cohabit with her husband. In May 1820 she was convicted of premeditated murder and condemned to suffer the nearest punishment to death – exposure to ridicule on the gallows at Tulbagh with a rope round her neck, followed by a severe scourging on her bare back, branding, and the obligation to labour in irons on Robben Island, without wages, for life.

Although the Court of Justice showed no pity, Henrietta's owner possessed a degree of compassion that was unusual for the times. Writing to the acting governor, Sir Rufane Donkin, Johannes Rabe blamed himself in part for his housemaid's plight.[31] She had always behaved well and would most likely never have been prosecuted, had he not purchased Saida – whom he afterwards discovered had been sold on account of her bad character. Being a slave, it was not in Henrietta's power to be legally married to the person she had the right to consider as her husband, and who had taken her for his wife. This made no difference to her feelings, for a slave who tenderly loved her consort, and saw another woman committing adultery with him, would experience 'a continual vexation of mind'. According to Rabe, this 'hurt feeling and heart-breaking' would lead to desperation and a resolution to remove the guilty object disturbing the peace betwixt husband and wife. In view of her faithful services and proper conduct, he begged Donkin to pardon his slave or mitigate her punishment.

6. The poorer side of town – noise and bustle in the Waterkant, a short distance above the fish market at Rogge Bay. Free blacks and slaves who had permission to 'live out' inhabited overcrowded houses lining the narrow lanes and alleys in this district. Sketch by Sir Charles D'Oyly, dated 17.4.1832.

Donkin, a desolate widower who was not generally sympathetic to petitioners, was sufficiently moved to reduce Henrietta's confinement in irons to a term of seven years. She served part of her sentence at the new drostdy at Worcester, and in November 1823 Rabe's widow transferred her to the landdrost, Captain Charles Trappes, whose widow manumitted her in 1830.[32]

Helping each other

The inhabitants of the Cape Colony had the right to address memorials to the governor, and the Cape Town Archives Repository contains thousands of letters from ordinary people asking for favours or relief. Some drafted their own letters, but those who were illiterate or semi-literate employed notaries (persons with some legal training who were authorised to draw up and attest wills, contracts and petitions) to formulate their requests in the approved excessively humble style. Some petitions concerned manumission – the only legal means by which a slave could hope to escape a life of perpetual bondage.

Although small numbers of slaves were freed throughout the 176 year span of slavery at the Cape, the tempo increased to an average of 86 per year during the period 1808 to 1834. Some were manumitted by their white owners, others – generally those with particular skills – worked in their spare time to 'buy themselves free', and a surprising number were liberated by their free black owners and kinsfolk. Urban slaves were the main beneficiaries: 92 per cent of the 1 245 manumissions recorded between 1815 and 1830 took place in Cape Town. Women predominated – they were cheaper than men, and the financial sacrifice was consequently less.

Freedom sometimes came at a price. Men and women who had never had to concern themselves about where to sleep, when to eat, or what to wear, were suddenly responsible for maintaining themselves and their children in sickness and health. Small wonder that the hire-houses in the poor districts near Rogge Bay and behind the Barracks were grossly overcrowded – people were grateful for any kind of shelter as they struggled to find their feet in a hostile world. Where jobs were available, they were often casual or seasonal, and without the support of the small free black community, many ex-slaves would have been forced into a desperate life of crime. Those who managed by dint of hard work to rent a room and build up a little capital, often used it to free other loved ones.

Prior to Ordinance 19 of 1826, those applying for deeds of manumission were required to pay 50 Rixdollars to the poor fund of the Reformed Church and guarantee that the freed slave would not attempt to draw poor relief for 20 years. Some free black families who had scraped and saved to purchase a relative could not afford this extra fee, and in such cases their kinsfolk remained slaves in the eyes of the law and had to be registered at the Slave Office. This denied them a sense of security, as they could be bequeathed against their wishes or sold to defray outstanding debts. When the law was changed there was a rush to obtain the coveted deeds, and 245 were issued in 1827. The Ordinance also made it easier for slaves to negotiate their own freedom, but market prices remained high relative to their earning power.

In the twenty years from 1806, free black owners applied for permission to manumit at least 175 slaves. Some were their own servants and journeymen, while others were undoubtedly relatives, including wives and children who had often been purchased in installments. Aploon Beyers paid Magdalena de Villers 800 Rixdollars for her granddaughter Sita, aged 16, and Regina of the Cape purchased her cousin Saartje from G Leeuwner for the large sum of 1 400 Rixdollars.[33]

Letjon of Bali freed his slave woman Simbar of Bougies, and Simon of Ceylon freed Minna of the Cape 'in return for all her good services and constant dutiful behaviour towards him during her bondage'.[34] Applicants named Fortuin of Ceylon and Fortuin of Bengal freed a total of seven women and a man during one two-year period.[35] Another Fortuin, this time 'of the Cape' was freed by his owner Roosje of Samarang, in 1811.[36] Anau of Java, who was blind, freed three slaves at once: Joemat and

Slammat of Mozambique, and Rasia of the Cape. Serina of the Cape applied to free Betje of the Cape, a slave she had purchased from a deceased estate.[37]

Seven years before her death the free woman Catryn of the Cape purchased a slave named Achillis of Bougies for 550 Rixdollars from JJ van der Berg, on condition that he be manumitted after her demise. When Catryn died in 1812 her son Abdul Soeker applied to free Achillis in terms of the contact signed in 1805.[38] Most of these requests were signed by the applicants with a quavering cross, but three Muslims and a Chinaman were able to write their names in their distinctive scripts. The only western-style signature is that of Hendrik Canterbury, a successful member of the free black community whose name is commemorated in Cape Town's Canterbury Street.

Despite these heroic efforts, manumission rates at the Cape were low when compared to other slave-owning societies. Many colonists seemed determined to reap the maximum return on their human property, regardless of years of faithful service and – in some cases – bonds of genuine affection. Owners who could not bear to part with their slaves in life were sometimes prepared to free them in terms of a will. Such deferred generosity was the particular prerogative of widows, who were probably oblivious to their slaves' secret hopes for their speedy demise. As was to be expected, the system was open to abuse. Slaves who had been promised testamentary manumission in return for sexual services or as an incentive for good behaviour sometimes found that they had been cruelly duped. Others imagined that their children were included in the bargain, only to find that they had been mistaken.

Romina Sophia Helena Jacobsen

In April 1808 an ex-slave named Romina Sophia Helena Jacobsen (also known as Romana Jacobse) petitioned the Earl of Caledon, complaining of the unjust and cruel treatment of Mr Constant van Nuldt Onkruydt towards her, 'when in a violent manner he deprived her of both her daughters, under the specious pretence that they were still slaves,' and informed her that she would have to pay 500 Rixdollars for their freedom.

Onkruydt (1745 to 1813), a prosperous merchant and member of the Burgher Senate, was one of the executors of the estate of his brother-in-law Pieter Juriaan van der Heyde (1749 to 1806), a well-to-do burgher and slave-holder. Van der Heyde was a reasonably enlightened man but he was not over-generous. His will made provision for special consideration to be given to three elderly slaves, and he freed Christiaan and Romina, both born in the Cape, in recognition of their faithful service.[39] The two deserving slaves were duly manumitted early in December 1806, and Romina was at liberty to make her living as a washerwoman while her daughters remained in slavery.[40] It is not clear whether she had been led to expect their freedom or whether her imagination had run away with her, but her disappointment was intense, and she submitted two memorials to the governor begging for his intervention.[41] Despite the double mediation of a notary and a sworn translator, her anguish and her passionate concern for her daughters ring out across two centuries. She also visited the fiscal's office three times to inquire after the matter, but could not obtain audience.

Attractive young slave girls were often at risk of rape or seduction – if not by their master, then by the young sons of the household – and Romina, who had carefully taught her children moral and Christian principles, was particularly anxious to preserve the innocence of her elder daughter, who was nearly fifteen. She continued: 'If your petitioner should prematurely depart this life, her wretched daughters, being then deprived of their dear parent's only intercession, would unluckily be compelled to continue for ever in that unlawful bondage!'

Her joy at being free was diminished by being parted from her beloved children, 'of whom she is as yet bereft in such a strange manner, that even on Sundays, they will not permit them a few hours to come and see their dear mother. They weep! they cry! but all to no purpose.' Despite her belief that her girls were being detained illegally, she offered to pay the interest on the sum Onkruydt demanded, 'until by dint of her and her daughters' handiwork, she will be enabled to discharge the whole'.

The governor refused to interfere, and her request is endorsed: 'The memorialist must petition the Court of Justice for redress, who will take such steps in her case as the law directs.' Romina must have known in her heart that this would be fruitless, and she set about raising the money to buy her daughters, who were baptised in 1814. She could not spare the extra 100 Rixdollars needed to manumit them, and they were living with her as her slaves when she died in March 1815. She bequeathed them all her worldly goods: two tables, three chairs and *'een kisten houdende alle myne klederen & linnengoed'*. This chest contained three chemises, five skirts, two corsets, four gowns, three nightgowns, a shawl, three head scarves, six caps, two pairs of gloves, and three pairs of stockings – a modest wardrobe, but one that marked her as a free person of colour and not a slave. Her daughters Johanna Francina Hendrina and Rosina Sophia were formally manumitted when her tiny estate was settled in 1819.[42]

Maria Fredrika Christina Abelbeek

In 1813 a strong-minded woman who had once been a slave complained to Sir John Cradock about the cruel treatment meted out to her daughter and granddaughter by their ill-tempered owners. This was a decade before the British began to introduce legislation designed to protect slaves from serious abuse, and her appeals were unsuccessful, but her petition allows us a glimpse of the experiences of two women whose lives were squandered in the service of others.

Not much is known about Maria Fredrika Christina Abelbeek (1755 to 1834), but she was apparently the daughter a slave mother and a white father, and grew up a slave. By the time she was manumitted by her owner, Hans Jurgen Botha, she had given birth to at least one child, a daughter named Marie.

Once free, Maria sought baptism, and in about 1810, when she was well over 50, she attended the first midwifery school at the Cape, organised by Dr Wehr, the colonial accoucheur, who was disturbed by 'the great want of proper and able midwives in this Colony'.[43] Theoretical classes were held at the doctor's house in Castle Street, and the women gained practical experience by attending confinements in the Slave Lodge. High standards of professional conduct were required, and certificates were granted to the successful candidates, including Maria. Her thorough training enabled her to make a modest living and put some money aside. Although she did not have the funds to purchase her relatives, she managed to maintain contact, despite the distance that separated them.

Her daughter Marie (*c.*1774 to1829) was a housemaid belonging to a farmer living at Riebeek Kasteel, and her granddaughter Abigael (b.1797) was owned by the widow De Jager of Swellendam. When Abigael was 13 she was impregnated by her former owner, a farmer named Lombard, who afterwards sold her to the widow to punish her for daring to complain. She was so badly treated by her new mistress that she applied to the landdrost of Swellendam for justice, but after keeping her confined for some time, he interviewed her briefly and sent her back home, where she was instantly flogged. In 1813 Maria asked the fiscal to look into the case, but the inquiry was ineffectual. She then petitioned the governor to direct that Abigael and her child be conveyed to Cape Town in order that charges of rape and ill-treatment be investigated, and justice done according to the law.[44] Her letter was referred to the landdrost and heemraden of Swellendam, who soon quashed her complaint. Abigael remained where she was, and by 1830 she had given birth to five more slave children – events that may or may not have softened her mistress's stony heart.[45]

Next, Maria complained to the governor about the harsh treatment her daughter Marie had received at the hands of her master, Johannes Gerhardus Lombard (1777 to 1847), one of 23 children fathered by Christoffel Lombard of the Swartland. After complaining of abuse, Marie had been removed to the Tronk for 15 days so that the authorities could hear her testimony, 'but instead of receiving any redress she was returned to her master, since which time she has again been subjected to increased ill-usage'. Lombard had locked her in a room, bound her fast and beaten her severely and cruelly with a riem until she was covered with blood, and a part of her flesh was cut out. Maria begged the governor to provide her daughter with another and more merciful master, or to grant her other relief.[46] Caledon forwarded her petition to the fiscal, who sent it to the local field cornet for comment. Predictably, her complaints were deemed to be unfounded, and Marie remained Lombard's slave until she died in 1829.

In 1817 Maria applied to manumit a little slave named Hendrik (5), whom she had apparently purchased for this purpose – possibly another grandchild.[47] He may have been Johan Hendrik Abelbeek (1812 to 1879) who was a ginger beer manufacturer in the 1870s.[48] Maria, who was a devout Christian, lived in a rented room furnished with her treasured possessions – including her Bible in its special box – and died at the Poor House of the Reformed Church at the age of 78. Ten bearers carried her coffin at her funeral. In July 1838 her grandchildren Abigael, Christiaan, Hendrik, Diana and Willem, no longer slaves but apprentices, were summoned to Swellendam, where each received an inheritance of 115 Rixdollars.[49] Five months later they enjoyed their first taste of freedom.

Lodewyk of the Cape

As Marten Teenstra noted when he attended a slave auction, slaves drew comfort from their kinship networks and were devastated when they were parted. British legislation introduced in the 1820s was intended to strengthen those bonds and promote family stability, but the odds were stacked against slaves who tried to live a normal life in an abnormal society. For reasons that will have become apparent, many slave offspring grew up without the benefit of a father, and the bonds of affection between a mother and her children were particularly strong.

In November 1827 Lodewyk of the Cape (18) complained about a beating he had sustained as a result of protecting his mother from abuse.[50] His master, a wine merchant named Johannes Jacobus van den Berg, owned more slaves than he required, including three masons, two tailors, a cooper, a coachman, a shoemaker, a washboy, some labourers, two cooks and several housemaids, and Lodewyk was hired out as a painter on a daily basis.[51]

One day a white youth, the son of Willem Boonsayer, accused one of Lodewyk's younger brothers of petty theft. Their mother made some inquiries and when she found the charge to be false, she exchanged heated words with Boonsayer. Instead of making an apology, the youth abused her verbally and would have beaten her, had Lodewyk not intervened and thrust him aside. Young Boonsayer departed, but that was not the end of the matter. The next morning his father called on Van den Berg and complained that his son had been assaulted and beaten. When Lodewyk returned home for dinner at noon he was ordered to call on Boonsayer, who took him inside, locked the front door, and beat his face with his fists. Not content with this, Boonsayer also complained to the superintendent of police, who sent for the painter the following day to answer a charge of assault and battery. Although Lodewyk explained that he had merely pushed the youth away to protect his mother, and produced a witness to corroborated his statement, he was sent to the Tronk to be flogged, the first time he had ever suffered such an indignity.

In his petition, drawn up by the notary JB Hoffman, Lodewyk asked the governor whether, in preventing his mother being ill-treated in so moderate manner, he had transgressed any law. He declared that 'tho' he is a slave, yet he feels the same natural affection towards his mother as Mr Boonsayer can feel for his son,' adding that young Boonsayer was the aggressor, while Lodewyk's mother was the offended person.

Hoffman concluded – somewhat unwisely – by asking the governor to adopt measures to enable the slave population at the Cape to enjoy the same degree of protection as was granted 'even to cattle in Great Britain, by a recent act of Parliament'. As was usual in such cases, the governor asked for a report from the superintendent of police, who declared that when the parties were summoned to his office, Lodewyk had behaved in a very improper manner and had no marks to substantiate the punishment he claimed to have received from Boonsayer. He was accordingly sent to the prison to receive corporal punishment as his master had instructed, and he had no grounds whatsoever for complaint. The fact that Lodewyk was actually protecting another of Van den Berg's slaves was of no consequence to his master, who automatically supported their callow and domineering white tormentor.

The lad's father appears to have been Willem Coert Boonsayer (1789 to 1857), a dancing master who lived at 6 Roze Street in 1827, in what is now the lower portion of the Bo-Kaap. During the VOC era, social occasions were usually celebrated by uninhibited dancing, but the British deplored such 'country romps' and introduced new and more formal dances like the waltz and the quadrille at their balls. Dancing masters who kept up with the trends were assured of a good living, but Boonsayer seems to have chosen an unusual career, given his prickly nature and hasty temper. He and his wife Susanna, whom he married in 1811, had a large family consisting mainly of sons, one of whom appears to have enjoyed exercising the power that many colonial children regarded as their birthright at the expense of hapless slaves.[52]

Dollie of the Cape

A petition addressed to Acting Governor TF Wade in November 1833, testifies to the bonds of affection that existed between a free black couple named Abdol Galie and Saartje and their son Dollie (32), a slave who had been apprenticed to a goldsmith in his youth.[53] According to the Slave Register, he was the property of the shopkeeper Carel Christiaan Schmidt and his wife, and could not be sold or transferred.[54]

In September 1832, a slave named Jannie stole two rings and a brooch from the Market Square premises of John Townsend, a jeweller. Before his arrest he passed the brooch on to Dollie, who was subsequently charged with receiving stolen goods, knowing them to be stolen. Both men were found guilty and sent to labour on the public works on Robben Island for three years – a hardship not only for the prisoners, but for their owners, who were deprived of their services.

According to Abdol Galie and Saartje, the widow Schmidt had already petitioned Sir Lowry Cole for the remission of Dollie's sentence, praising his former good conduct and enclosing written testimonials from

Mrs Townsend, owner of the stolen brooch, and other respectable persons who knew him well. She had received a reply stating that Dollie had not served enough of his sentence to qualify for remission.[55]

When the young man's anxious parents heard that Jannie had been discharged early they immediately applied for their son's release, pleading that his had been the lesser crime. Their petition was signed in Arabic script by Abdol Galie and with a cross by Saartje. Meanwhile, on Robben Island, Dollie was trying to secure his own release. His petition reads: 'As Your Excellency has been pleased to extend your mercy to the said Jannie, and as your memorialist bears an equal good character (before and since his confinement) he begs most humbly to submit to Your Excellency's consideration that he is a husband and father, and implores Your Excellency to extend your clemency to your memorialist, who was led into this misfortune by the aforesaid Jannie.'[56]

Through the years, many equally worthy pleas had been summarily rejected, but Abdol Galie and Saartje's prayer succeeded. The heavy paper on which their memorial was written bears the note: 'HE has been pleased to accede to their request and has given the necessary instructions for his release.' Dollie's return didn't mark the end of his parents' troubles, however. In February 1834, a sad little notice appeared in Dutch and English in the *South African Commercial Advertiser:* 'Absconded. Since January 18, my daughter, named Rogeat, about 15 years of age, having a mark above her right eye, and one on her neck; and two gold earrings with red stones in her ears. Any person lodging her in the Town Prison will be handsomely rewarded, and those harbouring her prosecuted. Abdol Galie.'[57]

Chrisje of the Cape

A significant number of slaves at the Cape of Good Hope were fathered by white burghers. Some acknowledged their illegitimate children and raised the funds needed to free them, but others didn't seem to care that their offspring were doomed to remain unbaptised, uneducated and enslaved for life. Mixed-race slaves were understandably resentful, particularly if their fathers were known to them.

Chrisje of the Cape was the natural daughter of George Fredrik Simon Geyer (1780 to 1846), an official in the high sheriff's department, and a slave woman belonging to Jan Andries Horak of 22 Strand Street. Geyer and his lawful wife Catharina had three sons who were Chrisje's contemporaries, but the gulf that separated these half-siblings was unbridgeable.

Horak and his wife Maria Margaretha, a daughter of the famous Martin Melck, were an elderly couple who owned numerous slaves.[58] Chrisje grew up in their household and gave birth to a son in 1826 and an infant daughter who died in 1828. Her striking appearance belied her lowly station – she had a fair complexion and red hair. In 1831, when she was 20, she had a young white lover who gave her presents and promised to free her. His surname was Christie, and he was probably a son of John Christie

(1769 to 1856), an Irish cabinet maker and former sergeant in the Royal Artillery, whose 'very numerous and helpless family' were often in trouble.[59]

According to Samuel Hudson, owners encouraged their slaves to take white lovers and prided themselves on the fair complexions of the resulting offspring, but this is too much of a generalisation. Slaves who were 'perfectly white' were liable to be less tractable and more difficult to control. Strangers might mistake them for colonists, and the only way to prevent this was to dress them differently. Maria Melck reacted swiftly when Chrisje began to adorn herself with the presents Christie had given her. She confiscated several large hair combs and would not allow Chrisje to wear the clothes he provided, forcing her to dress in her coarse slave garments instead. Chrisje was very disappointed and complained of ill-treatment to the Protector of Slaves, Major GJ Rogers, who advised her to go home and apologise to her mistress.

Chrisje was probably too upset to show the required degree of contrition, and Maria Melck responded by threatening to lock her up and sell her to a farmer in the interior. After a second fruitless visit to Rogers, Chrisje was so miserable that she stayed away from home until the fifth day, when her mistress had her sent to prison. A few hours later she and her child Abraham were taken by cart to the Twenty-four Rivers (near Porterville) and given into the custody of a farmer called Booyse, 'whose wife informed her that she will have the whole of her head hair cut off; as also that she will be transported to the district called Roggeveld, and there confined to hard labour'.

Chrisje was nothing if not brave and resourceful. She escaped while the family slept and somehow made her way back to town, which she was 'happy enough to reach'. By now her domestic situation was so tense that she engaged the notary and translator JB Hoffman to petition the governor on her behalf.[60] Hoffman, a member of the German/Dutch elite, was an unusual character. He had previously quarrelled with his peers, and he had a fierce sympathy for his many underprivileged clients. His petitions are logical documents written in a clear, flowing hand, but his hyperbole and lack of tact offended many officials and irritated the colonial secretary, Colonel Bell, advisor to a succession of governors.

Sir Lowry Cole sent Hoffman's memorial to the Protector of Slaves for the customary report. Rogers admitted seeing Chrisje twice, but said he could do nothing for her because she had behaved so badly. The combs were taken from her because Christie, 'a lad of most notorious bad character,' was suspected of robbing his own father and passing some of the stolen goods to his lover. He continued: 'Chrisje's principal and most earnest request to me was that she might be sold to Christie, who however, had no funds, and I told her that I could not compel her owner to sell her to any particular person, nor to sell her at all, unless she had money, *legally come by*, to purchase her freedom by appraisement.'

Colonel Bell and the governor took a dim view of the affair and dispatched a stern reply. Chrisje was informed that she had brought her troubles on herself by her misconduct and her liaison with 'an abandoned character', and she must bear the consequences. The Protector had done as much as he could for her, and she was advised to try to merit kinder treatment by better behaviour.

Chrisje seems not to have heeded this unpalatable advice, and she absconded again in June 1831. Horak put a notice in the newspapers stating that she had been accompanied by 'a young Englishman, pock-marked, with one eye on which he wears a green shade'.[61] She eventually returned home and remained the property of Horak's widow until emancipation in 1834, by which time she had given birth to daughter named Agatha.[62]

Six

Underclass culture

IN 1806 THERE WERE just over 1 000 free blacks in Cape Town, compared to more than 9 000 slaves. The term 'black' is a misnomer, for these former slaves and convicts were predominantly brown south-east Asians or locally born creoles, some of whom were virtually white. The community included a sprinkling of free Chinese, and its members lived cheek by jowl with a few urbanised Khoi people and a floating population of impoverished whites.

Slaves lived all over the town, often in make-shift accommodation. Purpose-built slave quarters were the exception rather than the rule, and many slaves bedded down in the attics, cellars and outhouses attached to their owners' residences. The women, who usually slept in the kitchen, were obliged to roll up their bedding each day and store it out of the way. Their few precious possessions were generally kept in chests or boxes that could be searched by their owners at any time.

A new category of subservient black people was added to the Cape's heterogeneous population in 1808. These were the so-called 'prize negroes' – illicit cargoes of slaves captured by the Royal Navy after the ending of the oceanic slave trade. They came from south-eastern Africa and Madagascar, and were neither slave nor free. They could not be returned to their homes for fear of their being re-enslaved, and more than 2 000 of these hapless immigrants were landed at the Cape between 1808 and 1816. Having survived the trauma of capture and the dreadful conditions on the squalid slave-ships, they were apprenticed to eager colonists for periods of up to fourteen years.

Seen from the corridors of power in London, apprenticeship was a benign means of integrating displaced Africans into colonial society and teaching them skills they could use to support themselves when their indentures expired. They would be fed, clothed and cared for by their employers while they learned to communicate in new languages and adjust to western norms, and they would receive Christian instruction.

Seen from the colonial perspective, the captives were a valuable source of unskilled labour, little different from slaves, and there was fierce competition to obtain their services, particularly from British residents. Prize negroes rarely received any formal instruction and they picked up what they could by way of example. They remained at the Cape after their indentures expired and merged with the working class to scrape a living as wage labourers. Many of the early arrivals became Muslims.

Despite its mixed origins and marginal status, the tiny free black community provided slaves with a support network and a model for an alternative social order based on a distinctive Asian-style culture. The Muslim faith, so accessible and inclusive when compared to Christianity, was one of its cornerstones. The number of converts grew slowly in the eighteenth century, but there were 2 167 adherents in 1825, rising to 6 492 in 1839.[63] Part of Islam's attraction was that it was not linked to their colonial oppressors. Muslims formed a relatively cohesive group who were proud of their heritage, and – unlike Christian converts – they had no incentive to change their behaviour to suit colonial norms, nor indeed to 'try for white'.

The imams

The men who sanctified Islam at the Cape and kept it alive in the face of VOC opposition were either *banditten* (convicts) or political detainees banished to the Cape from the east to prevent the disruption of Dutch mercantile interests. Sheikh Yussuf (1626 to 1699), the saintly man who established the first Muslim settlement in South Africa, was one such exile. He arrived in Table Bay aboard the *Voetboog* in 1694, accompanied by 49 supporters, including two wives, two slave girls, twelve children, twelve imams and a number of sympathetic friends, and was received with due courtesy by Governor van der Stel.

He was not allowed to remain in the vicinity of the anchorage, and was transferred to the farm Zandvliet, a sandy wasteland near the mouth of the Eerste River, which is now known as Macassar. The VOC provided 12 Rixdollars a month for their upkeep, but the men probably supplemented their rations by fishing in the rich waters of False Bay. Although he was not permitted to proselytise, the venerable sheikh is said to have encouraged Muslim slaves to remain true to their faith. He died in May 1699, and his grave on a nearby windswept hill soon became a place of pilgrimage. In time, a simple shrine arose that was altered and rebuilt several times during the ensuing centuries.

Visiting Europeans were often surprised by the strength and inclusivity of Islam at the Cape, and were impressed by the reverence that Muslims felt for their mosques and kramats. James Holman, an ex-naval officer, was at the Cape at the beginning of 1829. In his book *A voyage round the world … from 1827 to 1832,* he wrote:

> There is a Mahomeddan Chapel about two miles beyond Mr Cloete's, which has been erected on the sandy flats by the Malays for their express use, where they have a grand annual festival, which lasts three days, on which occasion

> they congregate from all parts of the country, but principally from Cape Town. They travel in vehicles of various descriptions, from the largest waggon to the smallest cart, taking with them a sufficient quantity of provisions to serve for the whole time they intend being absent from their homes.

Many Christian clerics were nonplussed by the lack of appeal that Christianity had for slaves and free people of colour. Patrick Raymond Griffith (1798 to 1862), South Africa's first Roman Catholic bishop, noted – with some irritation – that many had no idea of religion at all, but those who did were attracted to Islam 'and will not think of any other creed'. In January 1838, after a long and uncomfortable tour to the eastern districts, the Irishman visited the shrine at Macassar and recorded some interesting details in his journal.[64]

> [We] proceeded to a Mr Cloete's where we took horses and rode to a Malay Mosque [sic] situated on the summit of a hill, to which we ascended by a rude stone staircase, rather circular and partly cut out of limestone rock, by an hundred steps. We left our horses below tied to the door of a caravansary where the pilgrims who come every year from Cape Town and all around, lodge while they go thro' their devotions.
>
> Both lodging house and Mosque are at present deserted and we could only see the exterior of both. The Mosque has a small minaret in the centre and contains the tomb of some prince and priest of the sect. The building is square and low with a portico: the windows are screened within and all that could be seen through some chinks in the walls was some drapery. A curious sight, however, exits outside: graves covered with white cloths ... each has a round black stone at the head round which a Malay handkerchief is tied, with another black stone at the foot ... These white cloths (of calico) are renewed every year and we found some sixty or more rotten ones under each of the last white coverings. These graves, it is said, must appertain to chiefs or high priests of the sect: it proves great respect for the dead ... I plucked the leaf of a turkey fig tree from near the mosque and here enclose it, with all veneration.

A succession of learned clerics followed Sheikh Yussuf into exile, but details of their lives are fragmentary. Religious ceremonies and feasts were held discreetly throughout the eighteenth century. Slaves were denied Christian marriage prior to 1823, but hundreds were married according to Muslim rites. There was no prohibition against Muslim burials, and in the seventeenth century there was a *'Macquesaars kerckhof'* near the dunes on the road to Green Point. Leading members of the Muslim community obtained title to several small cemeteries near the Bo-Kaap in the nineteenth century, and today these are collectively known as the Tana Baru, or 'new ground'.

According to Samuel Hudson, Muslims buried their dead in a decent manner. The corpses of slaves were carried to the dwellings of their free black friends, there to receive visits from mourners.

> The body is laid out and covered with clean linen. The bed and room strewed with flowers and aromatic herbs and the place perfumed with sweet scented waters. A neat cover for the body is made of split bamboo and tied together with white cotton yarn in [the shape of] diamonds, some of which are very ingeniously constructed. This is placed before the door of the house till the corpse is carried to the place of interment attended by several of his friends and their priest. The corpse is placed upon the bier and the bamboo wicker work covers the body, over which is thrown two or three clean counterpanes which the followers hold down by the corners. When they arrived at the grave the body is taken into the pit by two of the attendants and the priest, who sprinkles the corpse with some liquor which is carried in an earthen or copper tea kettle to the grave.

Graves were generally dug deep and the corpse would be buried in a recess to one side. During the ceremony of interment the counterpanes were held over the opening and gently waved by the supporters. For many days afterwards relatives and friends visited the site to pray, strew flowers and anoint the soil with perfume.

The Auwal Mosque, situated on private land in the Bo-Kaap, was the first building legally used for Muslim worship in South Africa. It was inaugurated during the First British Occupation, and its founding imam was a prince from Tidore in Ternate, Abdullah Kadi Abdus Salaam (1712 to 1807), also known as Imam Abdullah and Tuan Guru ('Mister Teacher'), whose banishment to Robben Island ended in 1793.[65]

Imam Abdullah was succeeded by Achmat of Bengal (1750 to 1843), a fishmonger whose wife, Saartje of the Cape, inherited the Auwal Mosque property. Achmat was the spiritual guardian of Imam Abdullah's sons, Abdol Rakib and Abdol Roef, and he claimed to have given them an even more comprehensive religious education than he gave his own children. Their temporal guardian during their minority (which in those days lasted until the age of 25) was Abdol Malek of Batavia, a Muslim teacher and doctor, who died in 1833.

Despite their erudition, the two young men were obliged to follow secular occupations in order to make a living. Abdol Rakib (1793 to 1834) worked as a tailor, while Abdol Roef (1801 to 1859) became a coachman and stable keeper. It was not uncommon for free blacks to own slaves, and the brothers inherited two female slaves from their father's estate, Mawaä of Ternate, an elderly housemaid, and Rachbat of Mozambique, a younger laundress. Rachbat had a son named Maubara and gave birth to several more children between 1816 and 1828.[66] In 1830, Abdol Rakib was ordered to pay a heavy fine of 300 Rixdollars for not informing the Slave Registry Office that Mawaä and two of Rachbat's children had died. He pleaded ignorance of the regulations and pledged that the five slaves that he and his brother jointly owned would receive their freedom 'at the decease of both proprietors'.[67] The Registrar of Slaves confirmed that he was aware of their intention, and the fine was waived.[68] Rachbat and her four children were manumitted in 1834, just a few months before slavery was abolished at the Cape.

The brothers' lineage and spiritual gifts soon attracted a religious following. Abdol Rakib led his own congregation in the early 1830s, and when he died in 1834 at the relatively early age of 42, his brother Abdol Roef seems to have taken his place.[69] Meanwhile, their supporters diligently collected small donations for the purchase of a property that could be converted to serve as a mosque.

Free black entrepreneurs often lived hand-to-mouth existences, hampered by a shortage of capital. Whether this was so in Abdol Roef's case, or whether his religious duties affected the profitability of his transport business is not clear, but he was unable to service the loans and debts he had incurred and in 1838 he was declared insolvent. At the time he had occupation of a store owned by JH Wicht at 44 Buitengracht, which consisted of a stable and two floors of accommodation. He seems to have shared this family home with a relative named Ajoeb of the Cape, who was a mason.

In March 1838, the messenger of the court prepared an inventory of the contents of Abdol Roef's rented premises. This list, preserved in the Cape Town Archives Repository, provides a glimpse of the furnishings to be found in the household of a culturally significant Cape Muslim family a few months before the slave apprenticeship system came to an end in December 1838.[70]

Abdol Roef maintained that everything of value in the house belonged either to his children or to Ajoeb, and although these items were listed, they were excluded from the subsequent sale. He claimed to own just a few worthless items – two iron cooking pots, two water kettles, a table and two common chairs, a stretcher with a straw mattress, some iron, cordage and harness, the underpart of a cart, a window frame, some old bags and bottles, and a quantity of chaff.

Most of the furnishings in what appears to have been a kitchen and living area belonged to Ajoeb, including tables made of yellowwood, teak and deal, a chest, clothes press and bench made of stinkwood, a small glass case and a kitchen table. Other useful items included a water cask with a brass cock, a pickle cask, a washing tub, two buckets, a meat block, a chopping board, a hatchet, two copper candlesticks, a small iron pot, a skimmer and five chimney chains. Two frying pans, eleven iron pots and three iron ladles belonged to various unnamed persons, and a man named Gawie was said to be the owner of a trunk, a box and a mattress.

Abdol Roef's children (some of whom must have been minors) owned most of the furniture on top floor, which seems to have contained several well-furnished bedrooms and a sitting room. There were stinkwood and teakwood tables, chairs, clothes presses and bedsteads (one of which had white curtains); feather, sheepswool and grass mattresses; bolsters, pillows, sheets and coverlets; a rice chest, a cedarwood spice box and a teakwood and glass case containing 'Malay books'. Other indicators of

comparative wealth include two gilt-framed looking glasses, two china gilt cups, a copper tea urn, two copper smoothing irons, two lanterns, two glass candle shades, a pair of window curtains, a selection of china and crockery and a number of small chests and boxes.

The surprising number of items listed as 'belonged to different persons' may indicate that Abdol Roef took in lodgers to help pay the rent. Their property included two dozen cups and saucers, ten dozen coloured shallow plates, a meat chopper, and various containers and utensils. He also found room to house a square teakwood table belonging to Stancie of the Cape, a large earthenware jar owned by a free black named Brutus, and Abdol Wakiel's copper boiler.

Ajoeb was credited with owning a common open horse wagon, eight horses and a set of harness. Abdol Roef claimed to own only one wagon and four horses, while the remaining wagon was said to belong to his son Abdoela. Although Abdol Roef's somewhat shabby domestic possessions were sold for a song, his wagon, horses and harness realised about £34.

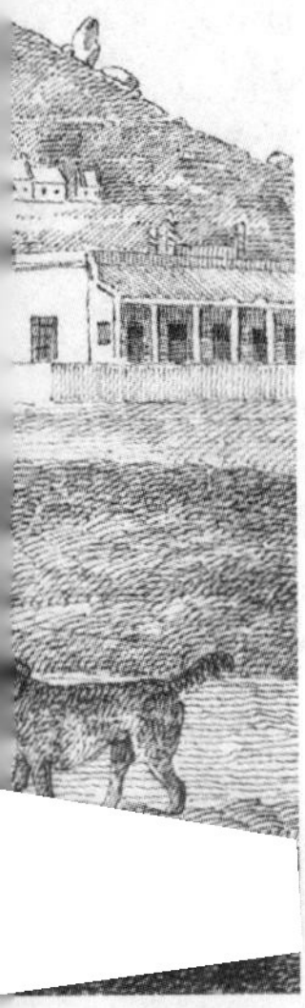

7. The road to Sea Point, an up-and-coming residential area in the 1830s, led past several formal and informal burial grounds. Note the Muslim grave in the left foreground. Sketch by Sir Charles D'Oyly, dated 22.7.1832.

Most of the proceeds went to JJ le Sueur, who held a general mortgage over the estate, but there was still a deficiency of more than £85.

Despite this setback, Abdol Roef's supporters continued to collect funds, and in 1843 they were able to buy a property at 39 Buitengracht for the not inconsiderable sum of £350.[71] The Buitengracht Mosque (the third in Cape Town) was inaugurated early in 1844, and when Abdol Roef died in 1859 he was succeeded as imam by his childhood companion Hamien, son of his former teacher Achmat of Bengal.

Christina of the Cape

In about 1801 a manumitted slave named Christina of the Cape became the common-law wife of another ex-slave, the tailor Tobias of the Cape. In 1808 Tobias applied for permission to cultivate a small piece of vacant land at Diep River in the southern peninsula, 'the nearest people bordering on it being the free blacks Abraham and Frederick, both of the Cape'.[72] Once the quitrent lease was approved, Tobias had his little farm surveyed and began to erect the necessary buildings, meanwhile continuing to work as a tailor in Church Street, Cape Town. Like most free people of colour, Tobias was hampered by a lack of capital, and his new enterprise seems to have placed an intolerable strain on his finances. In July 1809, he and his assistant Johannes Jepsen (another emancipated slave) were arrested and charged with fraud. As the sorry tale of their deceit unfolded in the Court of Justice, the intelligence, naivety and cupidity of the tailors fell briefly under the spotlight.[73]

Tobias, who had several pressing debts, needed to obtain cash without arousing suspicion. Several different currencies were legal tender at the Cape at the time, leading to considerable confusion. Tobias doctored a piece of paper money with a face value of 46 Rixdollars to give it the appearance of a note for 400 Rixdollars and gave it to Jepsen with instructions to tender it to an elderly free black by the name of Baatjoe, who had a shop at the back of Coenraad Gie's house, in return for cloth.

Jepsen had a light complexion and was sometimes taken for a farmer. When he had selected goods to the value of 52 Rixdollars, Tobias entered the shop and informed Baatjoe that his customer was one Croese, a Boer from Piquetberg. He also vouched for the authenticity of the paper note, and the old man believed him. Happy to make such a good sale, Baatjoe and his wife Cambang 'brought all their money together' to provide Jepsen with change. This consisted of some paper money, 18 Spanish dollars, a Dutch silver guilder, and 26 Rixdollars in copper money – a heap so large that they provided Jepsen with a bag in which to carry it away. The conspirators took their booty to a house near Rogge Bay that Tobias had hired for Styntje, his 'second concubine'. The rent was in arrears, and he immediately sent 46 Rixdollars in settlement to Mr Horak, the landlord. Styntje received part of what was due to her for making curtains, and Jepsen was given four shillings and the day off to enjoy himself.

On 4 July 1809, Tobias was informed by 'his girl who lived with him' (Christina) that Baatjoe had been looking for him as the note had turned out to be false. Tobias blamed the fictitious Croese for the fraud, but his story collapsed during interrogation by the fiscal. The tailors were tried, found guilty, and sentenced to be 'rigorously punished as an example to deter others'. They were to be brought to the usual place of execution, bound to a stake, and severely scourged with rods on the bare back. Tobias was to be branded, and they were both condemned to be put in irons and sent to labour on the public works on Robben Island or elsewhere, Tobias for 25 years, and Jepsen for 10 years, without wages.

Christina directed a pathetic appeal to Lord Caledon:

> Plunged in the deepest affliction, I throw myself at Your Excellency's feet and crave your most gracious pardon for my very unfortunate husband, the tailor Tobias of the Cape, who on account of an offence he is charged with, has been condemned by the Court of Justice to a dreadful punishment!

> Your Excellency will graciously be pleased to pity my doleful situation, as I have three living infants and am now pregnant with the fourth. Ah! My Lord, I entreat you urgently to compassionate [sic] my misery and to assuage the horrible distress of myself, of my children, and of my unfortunate husband.[74]

Her plea did not succeed, and Caledon confirmed the sentences. Six months later Christina applied to have the land improved by Tobias granted to her on quitrent, stating that she had to provide for three children and was reduced to the last stage of necessity.[75] Her petition was endorsed: 'Cannot be complied with, but in the event of the land being let to any other person every expense which memorialist has *bona fide* laid out will be reimbursed to her out of the proceeds of the sale.'

In 1813 Christina forwarded another petition begging for her husband's release on the grounds that she and her children had been in want of his support for four years and were in deep distress, but forgery was a serious crime and the governor remained unsympathetic.[76] Hers was just one of many similar tales of hardship, and it has not been possible to determine what became of the couple who once dreamed of becoming peasant farmers on their own small piece of land.

Jaria of the Cape

Browsing through the early nineteenth century petitions, one is struck by the cringing tone used by some notaries on behalf of their clients in their quest for justice or special favours. Although most letters follow the same pattern, forceful personalities sometimes lurk behind the stock phrases and the excessive humility. One such person was Jaria, a manumitted slave, who dictated an indignant letter to Sir Rufane Donkin in 1821, complaining that the Burgher Senate had erred in recognising her husband as a free man, when in fact he was her own registered slave.[77] This came as a surprise – surely Jaria should have been pleased at the tacit recognition by the town authorities that her spouse Absolon, a tallow chandler then aged about 50, was a free person and not a chattel? Not so, for she believed that this would seriously disturb the balance of power in her household.

Jaria and Absolon of Batavia were married according to Muslim rites. After obtaining her freedom she had worked – probably as a washerwoman – to raise sufficient funds to purchase his freedom, a significant financial investment. Then, in compliance with the law, she notified the Slave Office that she had taken transfer of him, and he was entered as her property in the Slave Register. She did not apply for a deed of manumission, however, as this would have made her liable for a fee of 50 Rixdollars, payable to the Reformed Church.

To Jaria's intense irritation, the Burgher Senate insisted on co-opting her husband into the fire brigade. Fires were always a serious threat to life and property at the Cape, and slaves were often suspected of arson. In the early days of settlement they were compelled to act as firemen, but from 1722 free blacks and free Chinese were enrolled in an unpaid compulsory fire brigade and had to turn out whenever the alarm was raised.

In 1799, a disastrous fire destroyed a number of official stores and stables in Cape Town, forcing the British authorities to tighten existing regulations and publish a list of burgher fire officers. Fire wardens were required to examine houses, chimneys and fodder stores for fire risk, and keep the fire-fighting apparatus in good order. When a blaze broke out, it was their duty to round up idle spectators and set them to work. Fire sergeants took charge of the pressure engines and supervised the free black firemen who fetched water, carried the hoses and supplied the muscle power to work the machines. Most slaves were excused this duty, for although large-scale owners were obliged to send some of their slaves to assist at the fire engines, the rest were supposed to stay at home to ensure that the fire did not spread to their masters' properties.

When Jaria protested that her husband was still a slave, she was summoned to appear before the fiscal, who informed her that Absolon was free because he was married to a free woman, and threatened to send him to prison if she persisted in defying the authorities. She was so incensed at this ruling that she immediately consulted a lawyer, who told her that Muslim marriages had never been regarded as legal either by the VOC or the British administration – something the fiscal would certainly have known. Next, she engaged a notary to draft a petition to Donkin, quoting the lawyer's opinion and citing the relevant clauses in the fire regulations of 1804. In concluding, she drew attention to the evil that would result if men were regarded as free after being purchased by their Muslim wives. 'No such wife would in future purchase her husband, in order not to run the risk of being deserted by him and to loose [sic] her money ...'

She believed that a woman who had worked her fingers to the bone to raise the funds to buy her partner needed to protect her investment. Once free, a man might drink or gamble or become work-shy – or pursue younger women – leaving his loyal wife and children in penury. A free man – especially one whose marriage was not officially recognised – could easily evade his responsibilities, but a slave who stepped out of line could be disciplined. The 'ancient practice' whereby such slaves were bequeathed their freedom after the death of their wives should be retained, otherwise many a poor man would remain in slavery 'who has now an opportunity of obtaining his freedom'.

Donkin, a career soldier, was mourning the death of his wife Elizabeth when he was detained at the Cape during a passage from India to Britain and installed as acting governor during the temporary absence of Somerset. It is doubtful whether he appreciated the subtlety of Jaria's argument. To him, it was probably just a silly dispute about whether a man who was to all intents and purposes free should be listed by his wardmaster as a member of the fire brigade. The petition, which ended with Jaria's plea that she be protected in her right as owner of her slave, is endorsed with the customary official response: 'Cannot be complied with.'

Absolon was eventually manumitted six years later on 31 January 1827, by which time the fee due to the Reformed Church had been abolished.[78]

Seven

Three generations of slaves

IN 1811, A SIMMERING quarrel between the eldest son of a well-known burgher family and his widowed stepmother took an unusual turn when he decided to support a belated claim to freedom by one of the family's slaves. Two South African courts found in favour of the stepmother, and in 1815 the matter was submitted on appeal to the highest British court, that of His Royal Highness the Prince Regent in Council. The background to this complex story, so far as it has been uncovered, makes fascinating reading.

Philip Wouter de Vos, baptised in Stellenbosch in 1731, was the fifth child of Wouter de Vos of Groenlo in the Netherlands, the founder of his line in South Africa. Philip farmed at Parel Vallei near Hottentots-Holland, and was one of the heemraden of Stellenbosch. In 1757 he married Isabella Wium, and during the next two decades they produced a dozen children. Successive pregnancies probably undermined Isabella's health, and in 1775, some months after the birth of her ninth child, De Vos is alleged to have asked his slave Francina, then aged about 30, to become his sexual partner.

Francina, the reputed daughter of Jan Pieter Wiemert, was partly white.[79] She had already increased her master's wealth by giving birth to four slave children: Mercuur, Steyn, Lena and Clara, 'some of colour and some white'. According to Francina's testimony, she was courted by her master, who wished to have 'carnal conversation with her on account of her mistress Isabella Wium labouring under a dropsical complaint'.[80]

She consented, under the express promise that she and such children who might be procreated between them should eventually be emancipated. When their daughter, also named Francina, was born, the child was said to have been treated, clothed and educated by De Vos in the same manner as his lawful children. Whenever Francina reminded him of his undertaking, he always promised to emancipate them after his death, and 'recommended her to be quiet on the subject'. He reassured her again when she assisted him on his deathbed in 1793, and said that she need not trouble herself about it.

Meanwhile, Francina's ailing mistress had died in 1779, shortly after giving birth to twins, and a year later her master married Femma Posthumus (1740 to 1825), a widow with several children. The new mistress, whose grandmother, Anna Maria of the Cape, was a woman of colour, seems to have been a vigorous and strong-minded woman. She soon presented her husband with his thirteenth and last lawful child, and there is every reason to suppose that his dalliance with his slave came to an abrupt end. Francina was free to find another partner, and during the next few years she gave birth to Rosina, Mietje, Joseph, Pieter and Levina, who were 'all white', according to her mistress. Their father appears to have been a colonist by the name of Heiniger or Heyneke.

When Femma was widowed in 1793 she and her eldest stepson Wouter de Vos (b. 1758) quarreled about the appraisement of the estate. Two members of the Court of Justice were asked to intervene, and it was decided to auction all the assets, excluding Francina senior, who was to remain in the family, but including the teenage Francina junior, whose father had not kept his promises.

Twenty years later the family was still at odds about what happened at the sale. According to Wouter de Vos and his brother-in-law Gerhardus Croeser, Francina junior was purchased by one Daniel Hiebner, who bought her with a view to emancipating her, because he was convinced that she had a reasonable claim. Femma's stepchildren were said to be astonished at the sale of their reputed half-sister, 'because it was well known to them that she ought to be emancipated'. After they had remonstrated with their stepmother, she asked Hiebner to return Francina, which he did for the same purchase money – 861 Rixdollars – under the express condition that the widow should never sell her again, but emancipate her.

According to Femma, she arranged to take the slave back at the behest of her stepchildren without any conditions. And so, as a result of her father's spurious promises, Francina junior became his widow's exclusive property. Slaves were not permitted to marry, and she had given birth to three illegitimate daughters by 1811 – the year she was sold, together with her youngest child, to pay her mistress's debts.

Francina junior had six maternal half-sisters, three of whom had been manumitted and baptised. Two were married to Germans living in Cape Town, and the third, Levina Heiniger (1795 to 1849), who made a living by fine sewing and ironing, became the second wife of Andreas Spolander, a Swede employed as an undertaker by the European Burial Society, after his first wife died in 1817.[81]

It has not been possible to ascertain which sister married Johan Hendrik Scheffer, a fisherman who became a gingerbread maker in about 1813. His brother-in-law Johan Christiaan Harms (1761 to 1847), a confectioner from Bremen, purchased Francina's younger half-sister Rosina Heiniger (1785 to 1848) some time after 1801 and applied to manumit her in February 1807. He wrote: 'Your petitioner, having got a maid-slave called Rosina, who very honestly served him for several years, is desirous

8. An early twentieth century photograph by Arthur Elliott of the old fowl house at Parel Vallei in the Hottentots Holland valley, where Francina, natural daughter of Philip Wouter de Vos, was born in the 1770s.

to follow the dictates of his heart by gratefully rewarding her faithful conduct with giving her her freedom.'[82] Harms, a generous, impulsive and somewhat naïve man, married Rosina in Stellenbosch in June 1807. He was a licensed retailer living in the Waterkant in 1808, and seven years later the couple were living in modest comfort in Keerom Street, where they operated a confectionary business.[83]

Femma's first impulse was to instruct her agent in Cape Town, Anthony Krynauw, to offer Francina and her infant Mietje to Scheffer and Harms for 1 500 Rixdollars. They received her proposal in March 1811, and although they had the utmost sympathy for Francina, they were indignant that she had not been manumitted after the death of her father in 1793. Motivated by anger and resentment, Harms accused the widow of overcharging them for someone who was tired and unable to work, and hinted that those who were responsible for Francina's predicament could expect divine retribution. He demanded that her older daughters Leentje and Rosina also be included in the price. The widow was not to be trifled with. She immediately sold mother and daughter to Anthony Krynauw for the asking price, and she subsequently hired Leentje (15) and Rosina (8) out by the month.

One of the strategies of the small anti-slavery lobby at the Cape was to draw public attention to the evils of slavery. It is possible that members of this shadowy group came to hear of the injustice reportedly done to Francina and encouraged Harms to bring the matter to court. They may also have helped him to obtain sworn statements from, among others, Wouter de Vos and Francina senior, to support his case. In 1811, Harms applied to the Court of Justice to be appointed curator (guardian) of Francina junior and her children, and he was granted leave to present a *pro deo* case for the reclamation of her liberty. However, the Court turned down his request that she be allowed to live as her own mistress pending the outcome of the legal process.

Despite their zeal, the plaintiffs did not have a very strong case. Although Wouter de Vos testified that he had heard his father say that Francina junior and her mother would be emancipated after his decease, he had neglected to make provision for this in his will. When Wouter declared that mother and daughter had been considered as free persons during his father's lifetime and were never treated as slaves, and that Francina junior had been instructed with his brothers and sisters in reading, writing and the rudiments of the Christian religion, his stepmother produced sworn statements from four of his siblings denying this.

Whatever he may have felt about young Francina's claims to freedom, Wouter de Vos did not take any steps to free her mother until after the legal process had been initiated. Francina senior was eventually manumitted with the consent of his brothers and sisters in October 1811, when she was about 66 years old, having given a lifetime of service to the family. She went to live with Harms and his wife who, having just one child, were well able to care for her.

In 1813, the Court of Justice ruled that Harms had failed to bring sufficient evidence to make out a legal case, and the Court of Appeals confirmed this ruling in 1815. Harms, believing that his advocate had presented his arguments negligently, applied for leave to appeal to the Prince Regent in Council in Britain, which was granted.[84] This extra-territorial legal process took several years to complete, during which time Francina and her children remained the property of their respective owners.

Harms was himself a slave-owner, but where his wife's relatives were concerned, he was far in advance of the majority of his white contemporaries in his appreciation of the moral and psychological indignities of slavery, and he took his duties as guardian very seriously.[85] During the legal process he tried to protect Francina's teenage daughter Leentje, whom Krynauw had hired as a servant to a Muslim ex-slave named Lea on the widow's instructions. Harms believed that it was demeaning for a girl with Christian connections to serve a 'heathen', and he offered to hire Leentje for the same price – six Rixdollars a month. His letter to Krynauw reads: 'I trust, Sir, that you will not refuse my request, because my wife is the aunt of Leentje ... and because I shall take care that she be further teached in the Christian religion.'[86]

When he received no reply, Harms complained to the fiscal that Krynauw had instructed Leentje to clean Lea's *schuytpot* (chamber pot), but in the meantime Lea had discovered her unwilling servant eating pork and sent her away. Krynauw then apprenticed Leentje to the Misses Mostert of Long Street, who ran a knitting school for slave children. According to Harms, they not only beat her for insolence, but ordered her to remove her comb from her hair and take off her shoes and stockings, 'altho' since some years she ... is not accustomed to go barefooted'.

Shoes – along with hats and horses – had long been symbols of white privilege at the Cape. The fiscal informed Harms that according to the Statutes of India, no slave was permitted to wear shoes and stockings, and warned him that his complaints of ill-treatment might lead to an action for malicious misrepresentation by the Mosterts. On 4 December 1815 Leentje gave her employers the slip and went to visit her mother at Krynauw's house. She complained to Krynauw that she had been locked up for many days without a bed to sleep on, deprived of her footwear, and given insufficient food, 'upon which she was turned out of his house and advised to complain to the fiscal'.

With a reckless spirit at odds with her lowly status, Leentje did so – to her detriment. Her complaints, which were entered in the day book kept in the fiscal's office, were: that she was kept strictly and not allowed to come to the street door, that she was not allowed to wear shoes and stockings, that she was obliged to tie up her hair, that she did not get sufficient food, and that she was not allowed to practice her reading in her spare time.[87] The fiscal sent for Miss Elisabeth Mostert, who replied indignantly that Leentje had never received a single blow in her house, and ate with the rest of the scholars out of the same pot. Their usual dinner, besides bread, was soup, meat and vegetables. She was made to remove her shoes and stockings 'on account of gross impudence and obstinacy to learn'. She was not allowed to wear curls in her hair because she was guilty of attempting to raise herself above her fellow scholars. She had recently received a visit from her mother on the stoep – proof that she had not been locked up as she claimed.

Her companions Nonnie (slave of Mr JA Truter), Leentje II (slave of Mr Carel Haupt) and Catryn Wintersteyn, a baptised Bastard Hottentot, all supported Miss Mostert. Leentje told the fiscal that she was unable to produce anyone to corroborate her statements 'because it all happened within doors, and everyone in the house are on the side of the accused'. This sealed her fate. In view of her 'unfounded false complaints', the fiscal ordered her to be beaten by the so-called caffers (prisoners employed to administer punishment) in the public prison. She was tied to a post and received 'twenty stripes with heavy rope ends' before being returned to her employers. There, she was repeatedly forced to sit down 'although she complained of her inability to do so without experiencing excruciating pain'.

Harms, ever the idealist, found this punishment far more severe than 'such moderate chastisement as female scholars do and ought to receive from their mistresses in private,' and complained that her reputation had been ruined by the nature and publicity of her thrashing. He wrote to Lord Charles Somerset asking him to grant Leentje protection, and suggesting that the fiscal had exceeded his powers. Instead of whipping 'a poor, distressed, abused and innocent girl', he ought to have brought her grievance to the attention of the Court of Justice.[88] He did not receive an encouraging reply.

When Anthony Krynauw died in 1817, Francina (40) and Mietje (7) passed to his widow Christina Heymericks, but they could not be registered in her name because of the outstanding law suit. Sadly, there was no happy ending – the Prince Regent in Council decided against Francina, and she died a slave in the 1820s. Her daughters Leentje (22), a nursery maid, and Rosina (15), a housemaid, were belatedly registered as slaves of the widow De Vos in Stellenbosch in October 1819.[89]

Harms had previously vowed to free Leentje if his legal suit failed, and both young women were manumitted four months later, apparently through the combined efforts of their loving relatives.[90] Their sister Mietje was freed after Christina Heymericks' death in 1828.[91] In November 1827 Harms purchased an elderly housemaid named Steyn from the estate of Wouter de Vos and manumitted her three days later.[92] She was his wife Rosina's older half sister, and he undertook to provide for her during her lifetime.[93] He also cared for their mother, Francina senior (Leentje's grandmother), whom Philip de Vos had taken as a concubine in 1775. She spent her last 24 years as a free woman and died in Harms' house in Keerom Street in April 1835, at the age of 89.[94]

Eight

Resistance and its consequences

SLAVES WHO HAD NO hope of manumission were understandably resentful, and expressed their displeasure in numerous ways, including mutiny, physical violence, arson, damage to property, desertion, laziness, intoxication and insolence. In extreme cases they murdered rival slaves or resorted to infanticide or suicide – acts of desperation that deprived their owners of valuable property.

During the VOC period punishment was always harsh, but that reserved for slaves was particularly brutal. Although the incoming British administration did away with some of the more barbaric tortures in 1797, capital punishment was still imposed for a wide range of offences. Prior to the 1820s there was no professional police force at the Cape, and the fiscal kept order with the assistance of a motley company of old soldiers and discharged prisoners who acted as *'dienaars'*. They were often German, English or Irish immigrants of the lowest calibre. The streets were cleared of drunkards by so-called 'caffers' – convicts and exiles under the control of the fiscal who were prepared to co-operate with the authorities in return for privileges. They also ran the prisons, assisted the hangman at executions and administered floggings. They were extremely unpopular, and the system was a thorn in the flesh of slave owners, who sometimes encountered their convicted slaves swaggering about the streets on official business.

Something had to be done, and in 1826 Lord Charles Somerset appointed a superintendent of police for Cape Town. He was Baron Charles de Lorentz (1795 to 1873), a British professional soldier with German connections. Police work remained poorly paid and unpopular, however, and problems of absenteeism, drunkenness and corruption were not solved until Inspector John King, an experienced British police officer, reorganised the constabulary in 1840.

De Lorentz was empowered to try minor cases involving pilfering, vagrancy and disturbance of the peace in the Police Court. More complex cases were dealt with in the Magistrate's Court, and serious crimes came before the Supreme Court, which sat four times a year. Theft was extremely common – many slaves sold stolen goods in order to acquire desirable trifles or finance their gambling habits – but other common crimes included drunkenness, assault, indecency, driving or riding dangerously in the streets, polluting the water supply, refusal to work and desertion.

Hundreds of petitions have been preserved at the Cape Town Archives Repository from owners of convicted slaves who wanted them back, no matter how serious their offences. Their reasons were economic – during the first two and a half centuries of settlement, there was a chronic shortage of labour at the Cape. Slaves were valuable property, and farmers advanced all sorts of compelling reasons why habitual deserters, burglars and attempted rapists should be restored to them, with varied results. There seems to have been no standard response – sometimes serious offenders were released at the first time of asking after serving less than half their sentences, while other owners were obliged to submit three or four petitions to secure the release of a slave who had almost completed his punishment. Long prison sentences appear to have been handed down when the government was in need of convicts for quarrying or road building, while at other times slave offenders were severely flogged and sent home.

Many slaves preferred long spells of hard labour in irons with their friends on the public works to a speedy return to their irascible masters. Owners often contended that their slaves committed petty crimes maliciously with the express intention of becoming convicts, thereby depriving them of labour and causing them financial embarrassment. In 1832, WI Louw complained that his slaves George and Dollie were so determined to get among the convicts that they stole trifles and accused themselves of wrongdoing.[95] He described prison as 'rather a comfortable life'. Colonel Bell was not sympathetic. His scribbled comment reads: 'These arguments, if admitted, would only go to prove that no slave ought to be condemned to hard labour, and if he cannot be hanged, he ought to be returned to his master.' Louw's petition to have his slaves released was refused.

Two years earlier a slave named Christian was convicted on his own confession of having stolen eight fowls from a hen-house in Papendorp, the property of JF Kirsten.[96] The prisoner requested Mr King (Deputy Protector of Slaves) to get him sent to work in irons on the roads, but to his great disappointment he was sentenced to receive 50 lashes instead. It is difficult to know how prisoners endured this sort of punishment. In 1831, a slave named Malodien was convicted of breaking into a house at Green Point and stealing certain articles belonging to the Revd. Freeman. He was sentenced to be kept in solitary confinement for three days, and then taken to the New Market Place to receive 75 lashes on his bare back with a cat without knots, and to be further imprisoned on a spare diet for fourteen days.[97]

White offenders rarely received such vicious physical punishment, and they seldom went to gaol for minor crimes unless they were unable to pay their fines. John Jeary was fined ten shillings for beating his servant, and James Ambrose, a policeman, was fined five shillings for assaulting a Khoi woman named Lena.[98] When Joachim Kannemeyer was convicted of assaulting PJ Gildenhuis, also white, by striking 'diverse blows with his fist upon his head, and kicking him while on the ground in Breede Street,' a somewhat stiffer fine of thirty shillings was imposed.[99] For allegedly causing the death of his drunken wife by repeatedly beating and kicking her, Thomas Davy, a former policeman, who was described as 'a hardened man', was sentenced to two years' imprisonment on Robben Island by the chief justice, Sir John Wylde.[100]

Corporal punishment was carried out in public, and in 1825 the Revd. Samuel Broadbent of the Wesleyan Missionary Society recorded the horrifying nature of the retribution that slaves and people of colour could expect.[101]

9. Two watchmen dragging a recalcitrant black offender towards the notorious Town Prison or Tronk in Strand Street, near the foot of the Heerengracht. Thousands of miserable captives were imprisoned there in squalid conditions over the decades, including the instigators of two slave rebellions. Slaves were also punished there at the request of their owners, including Leentje of the Cape, granddaughter of Philip Wouter de Vos, who was flogged in 1815 for making unsubstantiated complaints. The building next door is the Customs House. Painting by HC de Meillon, c. *1832.*

Riding out today, and seeing a number of persons standing near where criminals are usually punished, I drew near, and found preparations made for executing a poor slave, who was under sentence of death for having threatened the life of his master. The Dutch clergyman, Revd. Mr. Berringer [sic], offered prayer; then the culprit ascended the platform, and the executioner began his preparation, but before it was complete an official galloped to the spot, bringing respite. This was made known to the poor fellow, but I saw no signs of joy in him. He descended in sullen mood, as if he thought strangling better than life to him.

There were also a number of criminals under sentence to be punished with flogging and branding for divers offences. I was curious to witness the proceeding, and waited until two or three of them had received their punishment. They were brought, one at a time, to an upright plank, to which they were drawn up by a cord on a pulley, with their breast to the board, and so high that only with their toes could they just touch the ground, to prevent them springing to and fro. Then a person appointed for the pur-

> pose, with a bundle of elastic rods in his left hand, came, and taking one rod at a time in his right hand, laid forty stripes, save one, on the naked back ... These, however, were quite sufficient to make the back quite raw, down which blood first began to flow, then bits of the flesh.
>
> This part over, the flogger stepped aside, and another person took a red hot iron with large letters on the end, out of a fire in a grate close by, and applied the letters to the raw back, from which a steam arose, and a slight hiss could be heard, as when a coal is cast into water. Some kind of fluid contained in a pail, which stood close by, was applied to the part, and then the poor wretch was let down, and another was brought to the place; and so on ... but I did not stop to witness the torture of more than two.

Frederick of the Cape

In 1816, an impetuous youth named Frederick (19) left Cape Town on a white horse and rode via Stellenbosch to the Swartland, an area he knew well. His acquaintances greeted him hospitably, and he enjoyed himself immensely for a fortnight. His holiday came to an abrupt end when he encountered Field Cornet Smit near Piquetberg and was arrested for not having a pass. His horse was confiscated by the landdrost of Tulbagh and he was sent back to Cape Town on foot in the care of a 'Mosambique boy' (a slave). Tiring of the slow and roundabout journey, he escaped while his guard was asleep and made his own way home. At the gate to the New Market he encountered one of his uncles, who walked with him to the house of Maria Josina van As (1755 to 1835), widow of Arend de Waal, who immediately sent him to prison.

Frederick, an orphan, was one of her house slaves, but she did not need his services and had previously tried to get rid of him – with disappointing results. When he was still a boy she sold him to Mr Baumgardt, who in turn transferred him to WS van Andringa, landdrost of Stellenbosch from 1812 to 1814, with whom he travelled to the Berg River and Piquetberg. This interesting interlude ended with the death of his master in February 1815, when it was discovered that the widow De Waal should not have disposed of him, having acquired him on condition that he was never to be sold. The previous sales were declared null and void, and he returned to Cape Town, where he was rented to a succession of employers, an unsettling experience for an unwanted youth.

Godlieb Andreas Barends, clerk in the Commissariat Department, hired him to look after his horses. Barends, the grandchild of a German and a woman of colour, had lived with Jacobina Petronella Dianas of the Cape since 1805. She was the mother of his large family, but he did not marry her until he became terminally ill in 1833.[102] In March 1816, while Barends was occupied on Robben Island, Frederick 'had the misfortune of indulging in idleness'. Borrowing his employer's horse, he wandered through the country districts, never committing any theft, but instead receiving food by telling the people he met that he was the boy who had formerly belonged to Landdrost van Andringa – 'as was really true'.

Realising somewhat belatedly that his unscheduled tour had landed him in deep trouble, Frederick candidly confessed his guilt to the fiscal and begged for leniency. He was shocked to discover that he was to stand trial in the Court of Justice on the serious charge of horse stealing, and that the fiscal intended to call for a public flogging and three years' confinement on Robben Island. At the conclusion of the trial he was found guilty of rambling about with his master's horse and sentenced to be tied to a stake at the usual place of execution and severely scourged with rods on the bare back by the executioner. He was not sent to prison however, but was returned to his mistress.[103]

Knowing that all judicial punishments had to be confirmed by the governor, Frederick sent a petition to Lord Charles Somerset, mentioning several mitigating factors, including his youth. He denied having stolen the horse, which had in the meantime been safely returned to its owner. He had not resisted arrest, and had hurried back to Cape Town 'to testify his repentance'. He drew attention to his unhappy state, caused by losing his parents at an early age, and the miserable uncertainty of his daily life. He was deeply affected by the possibility of a public flogging, by which he would be disgraced in his own eyes and in those of his relations 'who are all an honest sort of people,' and begged that it be carried out inside the prison, as had occurred in similar cases.[104] Something in the slave's petition must have touched the aristocratic governor. Although Somerset confirmed the sentence, he directed that Frederick's flogging be carried out in the Tronk in the presence of the commissioners of the Court.

Frederick's beating did little to crush his spirit of resistance, and he was twice punished for theft and fraud. In 1821 he was scourged, branded and confined to labour on the public works for ten years, but he soon managed to have himself appointed a black constable at Simon's Town. He deserted in 1822 and went to Stellenbosch, where he obtained two pieces of chintz from a shop under false pretences. He was sentenced in February 1823 to be scourged, branded and imprisoned in irons for life. He remained the property of the elderly widow De Waal until November 1831, when she manumitted him as a free gift.[105]

Louis of Mauritius

For 150 years the restrictive slave system in force at the Cape prevented slaves from resorting to mass action to try and gain their freedom. Then, in October 1808, Louis of Mauritius organised and led a revolt in the grain growing areas north of Cape Town, one of only two armed uprisings during the slave era.[106]

Kinship networks helped slaves to endure their servitude and retain a sense of personal dignity, and those who had no relatives to provide moral and material support found their situation especially painful. Louis, who had been imported from the Isle de France (later known as Mauritius) as a three-year-old child (probably in or before 1780), seems to have grown up as a loner.

His owner was Willem Kirsten, fourth son of the influential German burgher Johan Friedrich Kirsten. Willem married Maria Catharina Grove in 1780, but the marriage ended in judicial separation two decades later. As a result of this, Louis became the property of his mistress. At his trial, Louis was examined about his upbringing and moral beliefs. He said that his owners had always treated him well and he had nothing to complain of, and added that his mistress had sent him to school for a brief period during his youth. Although unbaptised, he claimed to believe the Christian principles he had been taught. He had resisted conversion to Islam because his mistress had warned him not to meddle with intrigues, 'which I therefore did not do, and this is the reason why I have got very few acquaintances in Cape Town'.

Urban owners who had surplus slaves often allowed them to work away from home for a fixed fee. Louis worked as a *coolie* (a porter or stevedore), which gave him the chance to mingle with other slaves in similar circumstances. After her separation, Maria Grove hired him out to his wife, a free woman named Anna, who paid twelve Rixdollars a month for him. He moved into her home, which was 'beneath the balcony of Stadler's house' and near Windell's livery stables at 18 Strand Street. This arrangement gave Louis the companionship of Anna's kinsfolk and a considerable degree of freedom. He acquired three horses and hired them out to generate an income, and he helped his brother-in-law Abraham Anthonissen in his wine shop, which was next to the family home. Although one witness described this establishment as a *smokkelhuis* (shebeen), it seems to have been a licensed *pachthuis*.

Anna's household included her mother Philida, her married sisters Rachel and Coba, and various children. It is not clear whether Louis was the father of any of Anna's offspring, who may have been the progeny of a previous liaison. Anna was a grandmother – she had a married daughter, Silvia, who had children of her own – so she was probably older than Louis' estimated age of 30. She was the owner of an old slave named Oude Baatjoe, who had paid 60 Rixdollars of the 80 he owed for his freedom. At the time of the revolt he had permission to work for a person of colour named Fredrik Arendse at Diep River, provided he paid his mistress a monthly fee.

Anna's sister Coba and brother-in-law Abraham Anthonissen appear to have been the most prosperous members of the partly Christian household. Abraham was the fourth child of Ontong of Bali and Sara Cornelia of the Cape, freed slaves whose offspring were all baptised.[107] Coba, whose name was apparently Jacoba Steenveld, bore ten children between 1799 and 1819, all of whom were baptised. By 1808, Abraham was wealthy enough to employ a *knecht* (servant) named Hendrik van Dyk, who lived on intimate terms with the family. In 1820, he married Abraham and Coba's eldest daughter, Johanna Jacoba Anthonissen, in the Lutheran Church, and fathered nine children.

The picture that emerges is of a lively coloured family consisting of

Anthonissens, Steenvelds and others, living at close quarters in rented premises and co-operating to generate an income. They spoke Dutch and understood a limited amount of English. Some may have been able to read, but none could write, and during Louis' trial Coba was obliged to ask the widow Egt to compose a letter to Silvia in Stellenbosch, concerning her mother's fatal illness.

In 1808, Louis, the lone slave in this household of free blacks, befriended an Irishman named James Hooper, a ship captain's servant who was stranded in Cape Town. Hooper sometimes lodged with Louis while attempting to evade detection. As Louis did not speak English, his friend Abraham of the Cape, slave of Jan Wagenaar, acted as interpreter. Through him, Louis heard the surprising news that there were no slaves in Ireland. This gave him the idea that if his enslaved black comrades could be persuaded to act, they too could be free.

By his own admission, Louis had no particular influence in the urban slave community. His decision to launch the uprising in the Malmesbury district was apparently due to his acquaintance with a certain Jephta of Batavia, slave of Petrus Gerhardus Louw of the farm Vogelgezang. Jephta had formerly worked as a *coolie* in Cape Town. Hooper and Abraham agreed to join the enterprise, and the conspirators decided to incite groups of farm slaves to disarm their masters and bring them to Cape Town as prisoners on their own wagons. Once in town, they would take over the Battery and offer to parley with the governor. In the event of their demands not being met, they would seize the powder magazines, open the jail, and fight for their freedom. Louis would become governor of the blacks, while Hooper would hold high office in the new administration.

They decided that Louis, who was light-skinned, would pose as a Spanish sea-captain in an appropriately elaborate costume, with Hooper and another Irish vagabond named Michael Kelly acting the part of English officers. Abraham, who had recently deserted his master, would accompany them as their servant. Hooper and Abraham made a preparatory foray to Vogelgezang on horseback to survey the terrain and explain the plan to Jephta. Then Louis sold his three horses, ordered the rich new clothes that were required, and purchased two swords and two pairs of epaulettes from an English shop.

When all was ready, the ringleaders set out in a hired wagon drawn by eight black horses. They were accompanied by the unwitting wagon crew and two new supporters – a hired *coolie* and a slave deserter named Adonis of Ceylon. Provisions for the two-day journey included twelve loaves of bread, two 'boiled sheep hams', and three square bottles of brandy.

Petrus Louw was not at home when they reached Vogelgezang towards evening on 26 October but his wife Jacomina Hendrina Laubscher provided the 'Spanish captain' and the 'English officers' with lodging and a meal. She and her five children were completely taken in by the charade, but the Irishmen soon lost their nerve. They slipped out of the bedroom window during the night, pretending they were going to raise the rebellion on other farms, and made themselves scarce. Louis remained undaunted. Next morning he flourished a bogus document and announced that the fiscal had ordered him to bring the Christians to the governor, who would send them overseas and give the slaves their freedom. Jephta assisted him willingly, despite Jacomina's protests. Nine fellow slaves and a Khoi servant joined the rebels, and the party grew larger as the day progressed.

This was not a typical populist uprising. Most of the slaves who participated did so under the impression that they were obeying orders from the fiscal, and discovered later that they had been duped. Louis' mobilisation succeeded because his message appealed as much to the slaves' ingrained habits of obedience as it did to their latent desire to mutiny. The insurgents split into smaller groups and visited 34 farms in the area between Malmesbury and the Tygerberg, repeating their 'orders', trussing up farmers and their sons, ransacking their homes for arms, clothes, food and wine, and driving their commandeered wagons towards Salt River.

The whites put up surprisingly little resistance, and the slaves, although boisterous, were relatively restrained. An old man received a number of blows and was dragged about by his hair, and a farmer's wife was raped, but the rest of the women and children were spared. Some slaves tried to protect their owners' lives and property, despite threats of future retribution. It is difficult to know whether their masters merited this loyalty, or whether their slaves were too cowed to revolt.

The news reached the governor while the insurgents were en route to their rendezvous at an outspan near Salt River. Lord Caledon, a shrewd and capable Irish peer, was not unduly alarmed and immediately sent detachments of cavalry and infantry to intercept them. By this time at least 326 slaves and Khoi servants had joined the cavalcade, and more than 40 farmers and their sons had been bound and hoisted aboard their own wagons. Although no blood had been shed, there had been a fair amount of looting and damage to property.

When Louis arrived at the outspan, he fully expected to see Hooper and Kelly there, together with his interpreter Abraham of the Cape, but all three had decamped. This threw him into a quandary, because he had been relying on the Irish to lead the final phase. Thinking they had gone ahead, he advanced as far as Salt River and waited there because he did not know 'how to act further'. When the troops appeared, the slaves who had enthusiastically followed Louis' orders began to suspect that they had been duped, and it soon became plain that no instructions had been given for them to bring the Christians to the governor. Those who could, melted away, and the rest surrendered without a fight – 126 at Fort Knokke and 200 at Maastricht in the Tygerberg.

The four ringleaders were still at large, and Caledon immediately issued orders for all the passes to be closely watched. He was at pains to calm the fears aroused by 'the misguided motives of this ignorant rabble'. Writing to the landdrost of Tulbagh, he urged him to prevent local farmers giving way to false alarms and abandoning their dwellings, 'and thus, by their timidity, causing the very evil which a small degree of firmness would entirely obviate'.[108] The two Irishmen and Abraham were soon captured, but Louis escaped to Diep River, where he spent the weekend with Fredrik and Betje Arendse, the free black couple who employed his wife Anna's slave, Oude Baatjoe. When Fredrik heard rumours about Louis' role in the recent uprising, he sent a secret message to Field Cornet Colyn, but Louis slipped away and was eventually arrested by a detachment of Khoi soldiers in a wine house in Wynberg.

Faced with dispensing justice on an enormous scale, Caledon wisely allowed those who had been 'merely passive' to return to their masters after a stern warning. Four ringleaders and 47 others were eventually tried in the Court of Justice, and all but one were found guilty. Louis and Hooper tried to pin the blame for planning the uprising on one another. Hooper's evidence contains a number of lies and contradictions, but Louis' testimony seems more frank. He admitted that he had committed evil deeds in terms of his beliefs, but claimed he had prevented murder during the revolt. The Court condemned sixteen men to death, but Caledon reduced this number to five, and mitigated the terms of imprisonment and corporal punishment imposed on the others. Louis, Hooper and Abraham were sentenced to hang, together with Cupido of Java, who had committed rape, and Jephta of Batavia, who was Louis' contact in the Swartland.

Louis' wife and her extended family must have been aware of the conspiracy, but all the witnesses denied their involvement. Anna took ill during the trial and did not live to hear the verdict. She died suddenly before her daughter Silvia could be summoned from Stellenbosch, and her death may have been brought on by shock and distress. Several months after the public executions, a free black named Fortuin applied for a reward for apprehending Louis when he broke out of prison after his condemnation, apparently in a last desperate attempt to escape the gallows.[109] The fiscal corroborated his claim, and suggested that his reward ought to be larger than usual, in view of the fact that Louis' escape would have been 'productive of very serious consequences for the Colony'. The governor agreed, and Fortuin received 50 Rixdollars for his trouble.[110]

Meanwhile, 42 farmers from Swartland, Koeberg and Tygerberg thanked the governor for his speedy assistance.[111] Having always treated their slaves well, they were satisfied that they had given no cause whatsoever for the revolt, and they were proud to learn that during the trials, not a single slave had alleged a complaint against his master. It was business as usual at the Cape – until the uprising of 1825.

Arend of the Cape

Slaves absconded throughout the 176-year period during which slavery was legal at the Cape. They must have been desperate to attempt such a hazardous undertaking, knowing the harsh penalties that awaited them if they were recaptured. All runaways were regarded as dangerous, and bounties were offered for their return. They were pursued with considerable vigour, and were often shot or clubbed if they resisted capture. Slaves who supplied the authorities with information were rewarded, sometimes with manumission.

Some slaves attempted to stow away on ships anchored in the bay, but this was frequently unsuccessful. Others managed to survive in the peninsula mountains with the help of slave or free black sympathisers. Gangs of drosters who concealed themselves in hideaways in the Boland mountains were unable to live off the land and had to steal livestock and crops to survive. The most successful band of fugitives within the borders of the Colony hid in a system of caves near Cape Hanglip (now Cape Hangklip) and lived mainly off the bounty of the sea. Urban domestic slaves, particularly those from the East, were ill-equipped to forge new lives in the wilderness, but agricultural slaves who had learned to handle firearms on frontier farms and had some idea of the country, stood a reasonable chance of crossing the colonial border and joining mixed-race groups who lived by hunting, trading and raiding on both sides of the Orange River. Even there, they were not safe; deserters were sometimes recaptured after being at large for several years. A few individual success stories have been recorded, including a relatively late escape by a slave named Arend of the Cape.[112]

Arend, a mason, was one of ten slaves belonging to Andries Jacobus Burger (born 1785), who farmed in the Sneeuberg north of Graaff-Reinet.[113] In 1813 Burger hired him briefly to a missionary party proceeding to the interior, and his meeting with the Revd. John Campbell changed his life. Campbell, a visiting director of the LMS, deplored slavery, and his enlightened views probably gave Arend the courage to abscond three years later, when he could no longer endure his master's harsh treatment.

The journey across inhospitable territory to the Orange River took two months, and for 17 days he lived entirely on the bark of mimosa trees. Weakened by hunger, he travelled very slowly, and when he eventually reached a Korana kraal he was prostrated for a week and a half. The people treated him kindly, and he stayed with them for six months before moving to the Langberg to avoid the Griquas, who were said to be capturing and returning runaways. For the next few years he led an adventurous and precarious life among roving bands of mixed-race people, but he longed to be able to legalise his position and live as a free person of colour.

Hearing that Campbell was expected at Old Lattakoo (near Kuruman) during his second tour of inspection, Arend met him there in the winter of 1820, and they travelled northwards together before the fugitive resumed his wandering life. He told the missionary that although he was a miserable outlaw, he loved liberty too much to return to slavery. If the LMS would buy him from Burger, he would work at any of their stations until he had repaid the amount. Alternatively, if his master would consent to sell him at a reasonable price, he thought he could obtain sufficient elephants' teeth (ivory) to buy himself free.

By 1823, Arend, aged about 40, had accumulated a wagon and oxen, 90 head of cattle and a large supply of ivory. In June, the Revd. Robert Moffat and the Cape Town merchant and traveller George Thompson encountered him camped at the Matlhwaring River during the mass migration known as the Mfecane. He joined their scouting party and a few days later he fought at the Battle of Dithakong, when the Tlhaping, assisted by Griquas with horses and guns, drove back thousands of invaders.

Thompson agreed to try and negotiate his freedom with his master, but Burger, hearing that an Englishman was involved, 'stood out stoutly, a long while, for 4 000 Rixdollars' – more than double Arend's value. Captain Stockenstrom, landdrost of Graaff-Reinet, eventually persuaded him to accept Thompson's offer of 1500 Rixdollars, which Arend repaid by sending ivory to Cape Town. In March 1824, Lord Charles Somerset granted Arend of the Cape his freedom and remitted the fee of 50 Rixdollars usually paid to the Reformed Church, in recognition of his assistance during the crisis beyond the frontier.[114] Thompson and the outspoken Dr John Philip, head of the LMS in South Africa, stood surety for him.[115] Free at last, Arend turned to the missionaries to improve his literacy and have his children educated. He and three members of his family were baptised by Robert Moffat in May 1829, when he took the name Aaron Joseph. He was still active in the northern areas, trading and hunting, in 1851.[116]

Galant of the Cape

Seventeen years after the first mass uprising of Cape slaves was quelled in 1808, an insurrection took place at the southern extremity of the Skurweberg, a remote area in the Koue Bokkeveld, beyond present-day Ceres.[117] Three murders were perpetrated on the grain and stock farm Houdenbek, which belonged to a pious and reasonably prosperous farmer named Willem Nicolaas van der Merwe (1789 to 1825), whose 11-strong slave and Khoi workforce was given regular Christian instruction. This 'most atrocious conspiracy' aroused fears that British efforts to ameliorate slave abuse had ignited 'the fire of discontent at the frustrated hope of a general freedom' among Cape slaves.

Van der Merwe's most valuable slave was a self-assured man named Galant, aged 26, who had two concubines, one a slave and the other a Khoi servant. His body bore the marks of many severe beatings, apparently inflicted because he refused to kowtow to his master, or address him as 'Mynheer' or 'Baas'. Galant had complained to the authorities of ill-treatment, but with a singular lack of success. Each attempt resulted in another so-called 'domestic correction', and he was also sent to the prisons at Worcester and Tulbagh for *'slaan met endjes'* (rope-end floggings) for bad conduct.

The slave's deepest grievance was the loss of his child David, son of his Khoi wife Betje, who had died as a result of Van der Merwe's cruelty

when scarcely a year old. In his misery, Galant was only too willing to believe the vague and distorted rumours that had begun to percolate through the country districts concerning the abolitionist campaign in Britain. Van der Merwe and his neighbours had no time for abolitionists, and were overheard threatening to shoot their slaves and the first official who came to free them, 'all in one heap'.

Galant used his powers of persuasion to convince some of his disgruntled comrades to band together to attack local farmers and seize their arms. They hoped this would spark a general uprising, but if not, they planned to escape beyond the colonial borders, where other desperate fugitives had found refuge. On the night of 1 February 1825 Galant and three Khoi labourers assembled on a nearby farm belonging to one Barend van der Merwe (not related to Willem), whose slaves Abel (26) and Klaas (35) had joined the conspiracy. The ringleaders managed to distract the unsuspecting farmer and snatch guns and ammunition from his bedroom, but their plans went awry when he escaped into the

10. The village of Worcester some twelve years after it was laid out, showing the imposing drostdy to the right of the church. It was built at the instigation of Captain Charles Trappes and replaced the drostdy near Tulbagh. Water-colour by Sir Charles D'Oyly, dated 28.10.1832.

mountains, followed soon afterwards by his family, who stumbled about in their night clothes assisted by two maidservants and a loyal slave.

The six rebels then rode over to Houdenbek and spent the rest of the night in Galant's straw hut. They killed and cooked a stolen sheep and were joined by another four accomplices, the youngest of whom was only 12. At dawn, when Van der Merwe and a visitor named Van Rensburg left the house to inspect the sheep kraals, Galant and Isaac Thuys (19) rushed into the bedroom and seized two guns. Van der Merwe's wife Elsie, who was still in bed, jumped up and struggled with Thuys until they reached the outer door of the kitchen, where Galant fired at her, wounding her severely in the hip.

The scuffle alerted the men and roused another member of the household, an itinerant schoolmaster named Jan Verlee. Van der Merwe rushed back to the house and Van Rensburg attempted to escape on horseback, but was thwarted and had to ride his horse through the front door to evade his pursuers. Van der Merwe decided to parley with the besiegers, but was shot dead by Abel as he cautiously opened the front door. Realising that the back door was in danger of giving way, the panic-stricken inhabitants attempted to conceal themselves, but both Van Rensburg and Verlee were killed during the ensuing melee. Elsie van der Merwe, who had crawled into the bread oven, survived a fusillade of shots and was later found alive among the ruins of the demolished structure.

Having fortified themselves with brandy, the insurgents rode away, but the rebellion was about to fizzle out. Barend van der Merwe – wounded in the heel and still clad in his nightshirt – had raised the alarm, and a message was on its way to the authorities. As the news broke, waves of shock and horror swept through the farming districts, but there was no general slave uprising.

When Field Cornet FC du Toit and his ten mounted men eventually reached Houdenbek, they discovered three corpses and a grieving widow lying in bed with a huge circular gunshot wound extending from her left thigh to her hip. The bodies were buried two days later, and the widow, her four children and the other survivors, including Galant's Khoi concubine Betje, were conducted to Barend van der Merwe's farm for their own safety. The commando followed the gang's spoor to towards a cattle kraal, where a stand-off took place. Galant, who had a red 'blood flag' tied to his hat, fired some shots in defiance before making his escape. The fugitives were subsequently apprehended one by one, with the help of local intelligence.

Abel, the slave who fired the fatal shot at Van der Merwe, joined some butcher's employees and was detained two days later by a slave who was herding his master's cattle. Galant and Isaac Thuys were the last to be captured. They hid in the mountains for several days and were arrested by a group of Khoi who were loyal to the colonists.

Today, reports of disasters and catastrophes fly round the world in seconds, but in 1825 news travelled at the pace of the horse, and delays and incompetence heightened tensions and spread unnecessary alarm. When reports of the violence reached Captain Trappes, the landdrost at Worcester, he forwarded a dramatic dispatch to Fiscal Denyssen, his superior in Cape Town. Denyssen immediately alerted Colonel Napier, the commander at the Castle, and sent an urgent message to the governor, Lord Charles Somerset, who was away in Albany. Circulars were dispatched to all landdrosts informing them that the conspirators planned to destroy the white population and instructing them to consult the latest *Government Gazette* for their descriptions.[118]

Having sounded the alarm, Captain Trappes became uncharacteristically mute. The fiscal, a pessimistic man given to bouts of morbid speculation, was annoyed and complained that he was being kept in a state of suspense. Fifteen days after the murders, reports filtered through via the grapevine that some of the rebels had been captured. Denyssen was so exasperated at the lack of official news that he wrote to Trappes reprimanding him for his inexplicable silence after his first sensational report and instructing him to send an express reply.[119]

The location of the drostdy contributed to the delay. In 1804 the large administrative district of Stellenbosch was split, and a new drosdty, designed by the celebrated architect LM Thibault, was built in the Tulbagh valley near the foot of the Witzenberg Pass leading to the Bokkeveld, Roggeveld and Nieuweveld sub-districts. Although the drostdy was some three miles beyond the village of Tulbagh, it was well placed to serve local farmers and those living in the remote interior. Captain Charles Trappes (1776 to 1828), who was appointed landdrost in January 1822, thoroughly disliked the building and its situation. When it was damaged in a winter storm in July of that year, he persuaded the governor to sell it and move the seat of the magistracy to Worcester, a hamlet laid out in 1820 at the south-eastern extremity of his district. There, at considerable expense, he built a handsome drostdy more in keeping with his idea of what befitted a colonial magistrate. This sudden move seriously inconvenienced large numbers of farmers, and extended the landdrost's lines of communication with his superiors in Cape Town via Roodezand Kloof by some 30 miles. An alternative route crossed the Franschhoek Pass, which had been upgraded in 1824, but it was also slow and tortuous. However, Trappes was confident that a more direct road was feasible, provided the crude path over the Du Toit's Kloof mountains to Paarl was improved – wishful thinking, as it turned out. The terrain was extremely broken and difficult, and the towns were not directly linked for another 125 years.

When problems arose in a distant part of the district, Trappes was ill-placed to take effective command. He seems to have set off to evaluate the situation in the Bokkeveld with scant concern for the apprehension his report had raised in Cape Town.[120] To the fiscal's intense irritation, rumours then began to spread that the prisoners had escaped while being conducted to Cape Town. He sent an angry express message demanding to know the truth, and instructed his messenger not to return until he had Trappes' response. It was not until 23 days after the uprising that the fiscal was able to inform the governor that the prisoners had arrived from Worcester and were lodged in the Town Prison. Attention then shifted to arrangements for a speedy and decisive trial, and numerous witnesses were ordered to make the long and tiresome journey from the Bokkeveld to Cape Town.[121]

The trial was a showpiece designed to allay panic and show that the authorities were fully in control of the situation. Although Galant's testimony exposed his master's brutality, he was the instigator of the revolt and could expect no mercy. The most important question facing the members of the Court of Justice was how many others to hang. In the end, Galant, Abel and Isaac Thuys were sentenced to death and five accomplices were condemned to scourging and various terms of hard labour. While in prison, the conspirators received a visit from a party that included Marten Teenstra, a young Dutchman who was sympathetic to their plight, believing that an unjust system was bound to generate fierce resistance. Galant, who was chained to a block, showed no surprise at their arrival, and answered their probing questions readily. He was resigned to his fate, and was praying for divine forgiveness. Abel paid them little attention and continued to play with a child who was sitting on his knee.

It was customary for public hangings and whippings to take place in the district in which the crime had been committed, and elaborate plans were made to convey those found guilty – and the executioner and his assistant – to Worcester by horse wagon in April 1825.[122] Such was the alarm in the Bokkeveld that 20 farmers signed a petition asking that the prisoners serve their sentences on Robben Island and not at Worcester.[123] The sight of former comrades shuffling about in chain-gangs was supposed to deter others from committing crimes, but the petitioners feared that when they visited the village on business their slaves and Khoi labourers might find the opportunity of conversing with the criminals and form a new plot, 'the result of which would probably lead to great and new dangers'. They were also of the opinion that the prisoners' presence would remind grieving relatives of their irreparable loss.

Although he denied their request, Somerset's nerves were also on edge. Rumours had reached him that armed vagrants were at large in the country districts and that a great number of free blacks had assembled on the Macassar dunes to watch the prisoners pass by.[124] Fearing that the usual escort of policemen and armed burghers would not be able to cope, he ordered a military detachment to accompany the convoy and remain in Worcester until after the executions.

On Friday, 15 April 1825 Mr William Mills, the second under-sheriff, attended the prisoners to the place of execution and witnessed the melancholy events.[125] His report includes details of the conversations he had with the condemned men during their last hours:

> I take the liberty of acquainting you with the conversation that passed between me and Abel during the time he was under my charge. On the Wednesday morning he called for me, and particularly requested me not to forget to make his grateful remembrances to the Reverend Minister who visited him every morning in the prison in Cape Town.
>
> Abel said: 'I have to thank God, that, through him, my eyes are opened, and through his instruction I know that there is a Saviour, and a Christ, to save all sinners that will acknowledge their sins with a broken heart. I fully confess I am guilty, and am willing to die the death I am condemned to; formerly I cried to think of the state I had placed myself in, but now, thanks be to God, I am willing to die; – there is, I believe, a place prepared in Heaven for my soul.' When he came to the place of execution, he said: 'If a pardon was now offered me, I would reject it; I am willing to die, and feel happy.' Galant also desired me to convey his thanks to the Minister, for the comfort and hopes he had held out to him. The Hottentot Thuys expressed a similar request.

The heads of the three executed men were displayed on poles in the Bokkeveld as a deterrent to others who might be planning to revolt.

The persistent thirst for labour soon overcame the farmers' fears, and in 1829 and 1831 Barend van der Merwe, who had evaded the murderers clad only in his nightshirt, petitioned the governor for the early release of his slave Klaas, who had been condemned to 15 years' hard labour for his part in the plot.[126] Van der Merwe claimed that he had a large family to support and had suffered losses as a result of being deprived of a useful labourer. Klaas had promised that if his master secured his release he would once again serve him as 'a good and honest slave'. Not surprisingly, both applications were rejected.

Another remarkable appeal came from Nicolaas Wilhelmus Smit, who had married Elsie, widow of Willem van der Merwe, the owner of Houdenbek and the first man to be murdered. Although severely wounded in the hip, Elsie, the mother of four children, survived. Her marriage in community of property to Smit gave him control of her assets. In 1832, he complained that he had been denied the use of the slaves Achillis of Mozambique and Ontong of Madagascar for the past seven years, and urged the governor to remit the remaining portions of their ten-year sentences.[127] When Sir Lowry Cole learned that both prisoners had been Galant's accomplices in 1825, he had no hesitation in turning down Smit's request.

Deborah of the Cape

Pilfering was a form of protest favoured by female domestic slaves who wanted to express their silent disapproval of slavery. In 1831, a slave named Deborah of the Cape seized the opportunity to pocket a few articles from the shop belonging to Johan Philip Valentyn, the man who owned her sister, but instead of disposing of them discreetly, she foolishly offered them to a lodger living in her master's house.

Deborah had more freedom than most female slaves, for she was employed by the bread and biscuit-baker Johannes van Schoor to sell confectionary in the town. This enabled her to visit her sister at Valentyn's house in Strand Street. One day in August, finding his shop unattended, she 'bribed with cakes a little apprentice girl of 11 years old' to look the other way while she helped herself to 15 crepe and gauze handkerchiefs.

Emboldened by her success, she returned two days later and took a much larger haul, including 36 silver thimbles, 12 muslin collars, 9 pairs of silk gloves and 12 pairs of leather gloves. The value of all the stolen articles was more than 100 Rixdollars. She sold some of the handkerchiefs to Mrs Helena Briton, who lodged with the Van Schoors in Zieke Street, explaining that she had obtained them 'from a girl who sold such things'. When this came to the ears of her master, Deborah's chest was searched, and the suspect goods were handed to Edwin Moore, bookkeeper of the Town Prison, to be used as evidence during her trial.

This took place before the Chief Justice, Sir John Wylde, in the Supreme Court in November 1831. The stolen goods were identified by Carolina (b. 1819), a little girl manumitted by 'The Cape of Good Hope

Philanthropic Society for aiding deserving slaves and slave children to purchase their freedom', and apprenticed to Valentyn. She described how Deborah had removed them from a cardboard box and a glass case in the shop. The evidence was damning, and the jury found the accused guilty as charged. According to the *South African Commercial Advertiser*, 'On passing sentence, the Chief Justice dwelt with great force on the iniquitous conduct of the prisoner, in seducing a little child to connive at the robbery of her master. People of this sort, entering shops or houses for the ostensible purpose of selling cakes, should be narrowly watched'.[128]

Deborah had plenty of time to rue her folly – she was sentenced to three years imprisonment in the House of Correction. This was a recent innovation – prior to 1827 male and female prisoners were accommodated together in appalling conditions in the Tronk at the foot of the Heerengracht. In that year part of the old Granary in Buitenkant was appropriated for use as a female prison.[129] It opened with twenty women in 1827, but that number soon doubled. This historic building, with its

11. Horsemen, soldiers and slaves make their way across the barren waste known as Caledon Square. The pedimented building behind the spindly tree to the left still exists in the lower part of Buitenkant. Formerly a granary, in 1827 it housed the Magistrate's and Police Offices and the female prison known as the House of Correction. The massive structure on the right is the Great Barracks, demolished in 1903. Sketch by Sir Charles D'Oyly, dated 1.5.1832.

handsome pediment and double flight of stairs leading to the front door, still exists and is one of the oldest surviving prison buildings in South Africa, apart from the Castle. Women were imprisoned there for more than 30 years, but today few people seem aware of its former history.

Inmates were closely supervised by a matron and a keeper, both of whom lived on the premises. They were provided with straw mattresses, pillows, sheets and blankets, as well as mess tins, pewter spoons, and 'common knives and forks'. When not cleaning their quarters they sat on stools and were put to work to redeem themselves, either by coarse sewing or picking oakum. The latter involved unravelling old rope so that the coarse fibres could be used for caulking ships or stuffing mattresses, a dirty and unpleasant job that was extremely hard on the hands.

In August 1833, Deborah petitioned Sir Lowry Cole for a remission of sentence, stating that during the previous 21 months she had 'endeavoured by sincere repentance and proper conduct to atone for the offence which necessity induced her at an unguarded moment to commit'. Her health had suffered, and would deteriorate further if she served out her punishment, resulting in more misery than the court had intended. She affirmed that both the superintendent of police (Baron de Lorentz) and the Keeper of the House of Correction (William Henry Read) would vouch for her good behaviour.[130] Her request was referred to De Lorentz, who wrote: 'The conduct of Deborah has been invariably good during her confinement in the House of Correction and I therefore beg to recommend her prayer for the favourable consideration of His Excellency.' Cole took his advice, and her memorial bears the brief pencil note: 'Acceded to.'

Rachel of the Cape

Rachel of the Cape, slave of Michiel van Breda of the fine old Table Valley estate known as Oranjezicht, was two years old in 1816, the year that Cape slaves were officially registered in a belated attempt to stop unscrupulous persons illegally enslaving San and Khoi people and 'prize negroes'.[131] Some time after 1827, Van Breda hired her out as a housemaid to a gifted immigrant family.

Rachel's new employer was a colourful Dutchman, the son of a minister of the Reformed Church, who started his career as a soldier. Justus Gerardus Swaving (1784 to 1835) travelled widely and spent some years in North America and Britain before turning to literary pursuits. He came to the Cape in 1827, as interpreter and translator at the new Supreme Court, and he taught French to supplement his income. Swaving's first wife was a South American orphan of colour who died young. His second wife, Charlotte Louise Wilbeaux (1797 to 1871), opened a French school for young ladies in Cape Town that lasted until 1836, and later ran a boarding house at her home at 3 Roeland Street.

In 1833, the household included the couple's five daughters and Thomas Corder, a church organist and 'professor of music'. One Saturday in September, Corder discovered that six sovereigns were missing from a silk purse he had left in an unlocked drawer. He suspected that Rachel, who tidied his room, had taken them, but he had no evidence.

That afternoon, Philida of the Cape, another slave hired by the Swavings, asked Rachel to lend her the money to buy a pair of shoes, and was given a sovereign that Rachel claimed to have obtained from her 'husband'. The regulation prohibiting the wearing of footwear by slaves, an essential control measure in earlier times, seems to have lapsed during the last days of slavery. Philida duly made her purchase and returned the change.

Rachel had also done some shopping, and Corder could no longer suppress his doubts. The following morning she was taken into custody by John Pettman, turnkey at the Town Prison, and searched. She denied having any money, but he found a sovereign wrapped in a piece of brown paper and six half-crowns and some copper money loose in her bosom, concealed beneath her inner dress. Having been warned of the

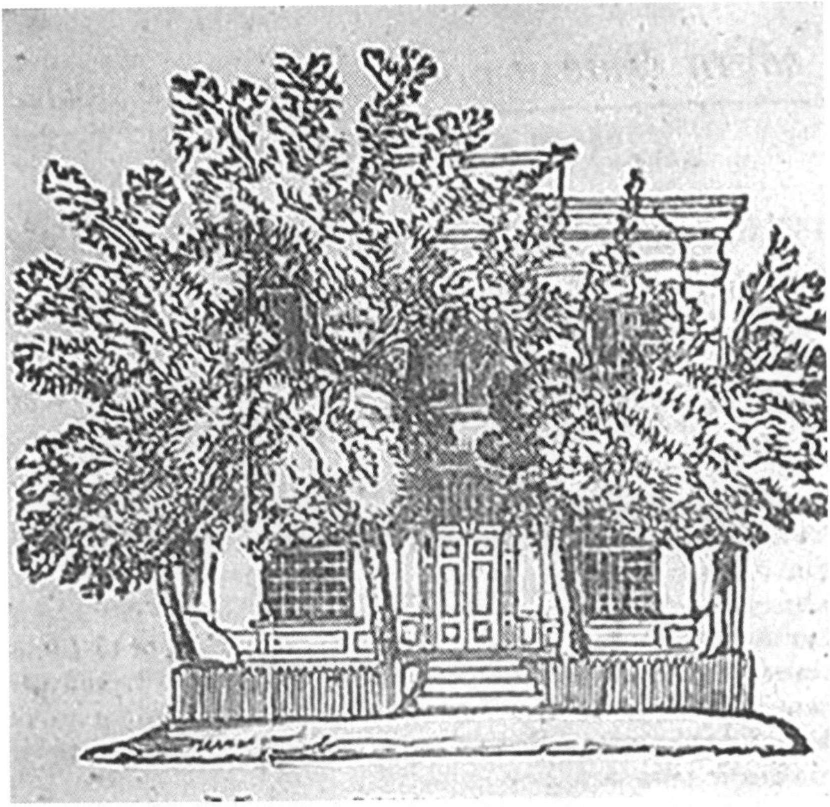

12. Rachel's home in Roeland Street. This woodcut by Alexander Reid was used to illustrate an advertisement for Mrs Swaving's French Academy for Young Ladies, which appeared in the Cape Almanac *for 1831.*

seriousness of her situation, she confessed the theft freely, and was prosecuted by the attorney general in the Magistrate's Court. She pleaded guilty, and in October 1833 she was sentenced to two years labour in the House of Correction.[132]

Although many slaves resorted to pilfering to express their frustrations, Rachel, aged 19, seems to have been a most unlikely activist. Van Breda thought so too, and in August 1834 he petitioned the governor for her early release on the grounds that her behaviour had been as exemplary during her imprisonment as it had been prior her uncharacteristic lapse. He could not imagine what her motive had been for the theft, 'as she did not appropriate to herself one farthing of the money she had stolen, but purchased ... several trinkets, the whole of which she distributed among the children of Mr Swaving'.[133]

Rachel seems to have been devoted to the young Swavings, who were probably more open-minded than girls who had been born into a slave-owning society. Van Breda ascribed her blunder to 'juvenile folly', and the superintendent of police confirmed that her conduct during the previous ten months had been very good. And so Sir Benjamin D'Urban sanctioned the release of Rachel, the slave who liked to make others happy.

Nine

Two sisters

Emilie's life of bondage

Transcriptions of oral testimony by slaves and ex-slaves are extremely rare in South Africa. Few slaves could write, and scarcely any slave-generated literature has come down to us. Until recently, the only Cape slave known to have been interviewed was Katie Jacobs, who was born near Malmesbury in about 1814. Equally vivid, however, are the recollections of Emilie Lehn (also known as Amiel Leen), whose reminiscences of more than half a lifetime of urban and rural slavery were published in *The Christian Express* in 1876, when she was in her nineties.[134] Her story is interesting not only for its content but for what she chose to conceal – unpalatable facts that did not sit well with the Christian precepts she and her family adopted once they were free.

Cape slavery profoundly influenced the type of society that evolved in South Africa, and its legacy is still felt today. By the time Emilie's mother Lea was born in the 1760s, every white burgher, no matter how humble his background, saw himself as a master, and few were prepared to work for others. From the owner's point of view, slave co-operation was preferable to resistance, and domestic slaves were incorporated into the household and treated as children throughout their lives. Paternalism did not imply protection, however, and sexual exploitation was common.

Johan Georg Stadler (1732 to 1800), Emilie's 'old master', was the son of a poor German shoemaker. He joined the VOC as a soldier and arrived at the Cape in 1756, at the age of 24. He married an orphan named Catharina Helena Haussamer in October 1760 and obtained burgher rights two years later. A tailor by profession, he accumulated slaves steadily, and in 1767 he applied to open a bakery. Emilie drew a distinction between this hard-working German immigrant and the boorish Dutch farmers to whom she was later sold. She described him as 'a pious and faithful man, who did good to us and treated us kindly in his house as long as he lived'.

Stadler was far from being the benign old gentleman Emilie described, but she was probably looking back nostalgically to her relatively privileged urban childhood. She must have known that he took sexual advantage of his female slaves after his wife died, and that her older half-sister Steyntje had given birth to his illegitimate child, but she concealed these unpalatable truths during her interview, which was transcribed and published in a missionary journal. Here, 'taken verbatim from her lips', Emilie describes how Stadler and his young wife Catharina acquired their wealth.

> They commenced their household in the most modest way in a hired room, furnished with the most needed furniture. Both feared the Lord and could work hard. They were never ashamed of any manual labour. He found work on board the ships lying in the bay, and brought home many things, which they had given him there as worthless or for a low price, and which he converted into money on shore. He attended the market every morning and sold these things to the Dutch farmers who had to bring their produce from the whole country to Cape Town. He made a good bargain especially with empty bottles, which were in those days a rare article among the farmers. At first he carried these things in a basket, but after a short time, he was able to keep a shop. He succeeded after a few years by his activity and faithfulness, in buying a large and roomy house in the midst of Cape Town, and in adding some plots of ground in the suburbs. He had a share in the lime kiln at Kalk Bay [it was actually situated between Roodebloem and Zonnebloem] where he employed one of his sons. He was not only blessed with riches but children to the number of eight, mostly boys.
>
> My mother as far back as she can think of, was in his house, though she does not know how she came there. Of course, she was a bought slave. My mother was nearly of the same age as the Stadler's oldest son [born in 1763] and grew up with the children of the house, and was called Lea. She behaved well, and even learnt to read. Whether she was instructed in it, or whether she learnt it from the children, I cannot say.

Lea of the Cape seems to have been of mixed Asian and European descent. According to Emilie, she was of good stature, light of colour, had long hair, and nearly European features. 'Mrs Stadler instructed her in all household duties and found her to be a good pupil. It was a very busy time. All labour in the house and on the farm was done by slaves, and again all slaves had to be provided for from home. There was much baking, slaughtering and cooking … Eight female slaves alone were daily busy with doing the housework.'

At New Year all the slaves were given new clothes for summer and winter. They were allowed to go into Stadler's shop and select the material they liked best, which was then made into traditional slave garments by two hired tailors.

Lea had a room to herself in an outhouse, where she was visited by a German who fathered several of her children. He died when their daughters Steyntje and Pamela were quite young. Emilie's father was a Frenchman named De Lettre who had come to the Cape as a soldier. According to Emilie, she was born in Stadler's large house in Bree Street on 13 October

1783, but it may have been a year or two later – her chronology is rather muddled. She recalled: 'When I was about 3 years old, my mother took me on a certain day to the upper story of the house, opened the windows, and pointed my attention to a vessel which had just weighed anchor. It was a man-of-war that lay grand and majestically before us. Soon, sails were spread and the ship glided away on the blue waters. When it vanished from our sight, my mother said: "There goes your father in the ship." We saw him no more.'

In 1785 Stadler suffered a heavy blow 'when the Lord suddenly took away his active wife'. Lea was then in her early twenties, and the entire responsibility for running the house and raising the children fell on her shoulders. Like many slave owners, Stadler indulged his house-born slave children, and his apparent benevolence gave Emilie and her siblings a false sense of security. She remembered that he was very friendly and enjoyed their happiness and play.

> Fruit and other sweet things he brought to us, but he never thought of sending us to school, for in those days schools for coloured children did not exist.
>
> It was a fixed rule with our mother in the evening ... to gather us round her and to read to us a portion of a religious book. Of course, it happened often, when we were still very young, that one or other of us became sleepy during the reading, and had to be awakened. Our mother taught us also to pray, and these prayers, especially the Lord's Prayer, I never forgot.
>
> In our little dwelling everything was plain but clean and in good order, so that we felt ourselves comfortable in it. If our lives had proceeded always in this way, we would never have known what a bad lot it is to be born as slaves.

This artificially rosy picture belies the awful reality of her sister Steyntje's life, which will be related in due course. In June 1800 Emilie had to put her childhood behind her and face the cruel reality of her situation.

> The hour of death came for our old master. He took the most earnest care for the salvation of his soul. For instance, when he intended to go to the Lord's supper he abstained for many days from all earthly cares, locked himself up in his room and prepared himself for the solemn act by praying and reading. His end was peace. He was buried in the Lutheran grave-yard in Cape Town near his late wife.
>
> What change awaited us now? What future was before us? In what state of mind was my mother, who had been accustomed ... to be, so-to-say, the mistress of this great household, and now? Our peaceful living together came at once to an end.

Stadler's death broke the kinship ties that had comforted and supported his slaves. Lea, Emilie and one of her brothers were bequeathed to his eldest son, a boorish young man. 'The quiet Godfearing way of our old master was not that of his son; he liked the pleasures of this world. One

Sunday [in 1802] he with some friends hired a boat, taking with them a great quantity of drink.' The drunken sailors were unable to steer the boat, which capsised, drowning young Stadler. 'The young widow, who had many visitors, married a Dutchman. He understood better how to spend than to earn, for after about three years the property was gone [and] one slave after another had to sold by him, to save himself. The hour came when I had to part with my mother. A Boer from George, who had come with his produce to town, bought me for £75 and brought me to his farm ...'

This transfer seems to have taken place in about 1808, soon after the oceanic slave trade was abolished in the British Empire. Every urban slave dreaded the possibility of being parted from everything that was familiar and sold up-country, and nearly 70 years later Emilie exclaimed:

> How many tears have been shed, how many groans raised on this fountain of sorrow by us slaves! Many an evening after the labour of the day was finished,

13. Avontuur, the mission village in the Langkloof where the ex-slave Emilie Lehn was living when her husband Hans drowned in the Malgas River in 1848. Although this drawing by JA Avis dates to 1875, progress was slow in the remote country districts and little would have changed in the intervening period. Emilie spent her formative years in Cape Town but was sold up-country in about 1808.

I looked for a quiet place to weep over my family, who were now far from me.

My way went through many thorns and thistles. My new master lived after the word: Let us eat and drink, for tomorrow we die. The farm was kept in good order, but the spirit reigning there was an evil one. Besides cultivating the ground, waggon-making was carried on in this place.

Her owner, Johannes Hermanus Terblans (1758 to 1827), was a hard task-master. At daybreak, when the cock crowed, 'the farmer cried with all his might out of his sleeping room: "Ring the bell, let the people rise."' If the cock did not wake early enough, he went out and pinched the sleepy rooster, which crowed obligingly. 'The bell-ringer made haste and soon the whole farm was like an anthill. Everyone knew his work and had punctually to do it until late in the evening. Only on Sunday afternoon, after everything had been cleaned and put in its place, the female slaves could do with their time, what they liked. No thought for their spiritual welfare came into the farmer's mind.'

Terblans owned 18 slaves when compulsory registration was introduced in 1816, including one elderly Batavian, three who were born in Mozambique and fourteen who were 'of the Cape', including Amiel (31), a housemaid.[135]

She recalled:

> Many years we had lived this way like burdened asses, when my master bought a so-called 'Bastard German', a clever and industrious man, a jack of all trades. Hans Lehn was one year younger than I. We were pleased with each other. He took me as his wife, when I was already 31 years old. Hans built in his spare time a cottage for ourselves. In the evenings he made scoops, whips etc, the proceeds of which were a great help to us. We had children, 3 boys and 3 girls, of whom the two eldest are alive.

Emilie gave birth to six children between 1818 and 1831, four of whom died young. Terblans died in October 1827, and eight months later the slave family was transferred to a relative by marriage, Philippus Rudolphus Botha (1771 to 1833), who farmed near the Cango caves in the Oudtshoorn district and owned a large contingent of slaves.[136]

The Lehns had already lost one son, Hans (b. 1822), who wandered into the forest near George and was never found. According to Emilie, 'a year later a rumour spread that a mad female slave who had fled from her master had stolen and drowned the child in a pool of water, but the truth of this rumour we could not find out ... We slaves had no time to watch our children properly. They were left to themselves, and thus it occurred that my little daughter [Steyntje], one and a half years old, in following other children jumping over a watercourse, missed the other side, fell into the course and was drowned.'

After living for some years 'partly in peace, partly in sadness,' their master died, and everything had to be sold. In January 1834, after serving five different masters, Emilie was put up for auction.

> There I stood with my husband and my two children on the table. The boy must be sold alone, cried out one voice. One bid, another bid, another, the hammer fell, and my son had a master; he must part with us and go far away. 'A man, a woman and a girl, what's the bid?' The hammer fell. 'Who is the owner of these creatures?' '[A farmer] in Dieprivier, Langkloof.' The Lord be praised, thought each of us in getting down from the table, that we are bought by one master. A new way had to be walked over, but in the old manner.

That was how Emilie remembered the sale 42 years later, but the Slave Registers for George show that Hans (46), a woodcutter, Amiel (48), a housemaid, Piet (15), Kristien (13) and Coenraad (8) were all transferred on the same day to Ignatius Marthinus van Rooyen (1809 to 1888) of the farm Grootfontein, who owned no other slaves.[137] The parting with Piet probably occurred when he was hired out to another master.

To be sold at auction was a traumatic and demeaning experience, but emancipation was approaching and Hans Lehn had already begun to accumulate the resources he would need for an independent life. He was thus able to negotiate a better life for Emilie. 'My husband was very excited when he found himself nearly separated from his wife, and although reports of the intended liberation had already come to our ears, he wished to be on the safe side and offered to the farmer his best two oxen for my liberation. By his industry he had earned a waggon and a span of bullocks. The farmer agreed. My husband remained a slave and I was free.'

This transaction was no more than an interim arrangement between the slave-owner and his illiterate slave. It was not noted in the Slave Register, and Van Rooyen received government compensation for all five members of the Lehn family after emancipation.[138] According to the records they were valued as follows: Hans (£195); Amiel (£90); Piet (£127); Christien (£90); Coenraad (£71) – a total of £573, but the initial assessments were later reduced and Van Rooyen would have received considerably less.

According to Emilie, a free man of colour named Piet Koen (1814 to 1862) made the acquaintance of her daughter Christine and bought her free and married her, but he probably negotiated her release from her four-year apprenticeship. Their first child, Pieter Matthew Koen, was born in January 1839, six weeks after the apprentices were liberated. Emilie celebrated the day in a very sober fashion: 'I was not able to rejoice in a loud and wild manner, as many slaves did. I thanked the Lord that he had freed our race from this earthly bondage and prayed to him to free us from the bondage of Satan. We did not stay any longer on the wild dancing places of v. R[ooyen]; we hired from another farmer a piece of ground which my husband cultivated for our livelihood.' Their son Piet (b. 1818) went to George and worked as a post-rider before moving to a place of his own near Plettenberg Bay. Emilie never forgot the Christian teachings she had learned at Lea's knee, and a chance conversation with a Moravian missionary who outspanned near her cottage set her on the path to conversion. 'The Lord blessed the words of this man,' she later recalled, '[and] my heart was opened.'

Although she seems never to have seen her mother, Lea, again after their cruel separation, Emilie had the comfort of knowing that she had been baptised. When Lea was due to be sold in 1808, her plight came to the attention of a farmer's wife who had known her when she was housekeeper to the Stadler family. The woman persuaded her husband to buy the slave and take her to their farm in the Caledon district. There she was kindly treated and encouraged to receive Christian instruction prior to baptism. Finding it painful to see 'her friend and sister in the Lord still a slave', her pious mistress arranged for her liberation. In gratitude, Lea remained in the household for the rest of her life and nursed the farmer's wife during recurrent bouts of ill health. She sometimes saw her children on the rare occasions when her benefactress visited Cape Town by wagon. Many ex-slaves, particularly the elderly, were ill-pre-

pared for liberation and soon swelled the ranks of the urban and rural poor. The knowledge that her mother had found a safe haven in her old age was a comfort to Emilie.

The Lehns made good use of their skills and were able to sustain an independent existence. The church played a pivotal role in their lives, and within two years their desire for baptism was fulfilled by a neighbouring missionary. Emilie recalled: 'Our daughter Christine, whose husband lived already on the mission station Avontuur [in the Langkloof] was baptised with us, and I and my husband married. We removed to Avontuur, to have an opportunity of regularly attending church and its means of grace.'

Emilie was widowed in April 1848 when Hans drowned in the Malgas River. He had taken his oxen across the mountains to Plettenberg Bay to plough his son Piet's land, and was returning on horseback when the river suddenly came down in flood. He was buried on the mission station at Pacaltsdorp, near George. She said sadly: 'So was my old and faithful

14. The young people behind (L) are the brother and sister Hettie and Gerhard Kuhn, great grandchildren of the emancipated slaves Emilie and Hans Lehn. Their mother Maria and stepfather Rasmus Jensen of the Berlin Missionary Society are seated in front with their son Siegfried, and the three young women grouped round Rasmus are their daughters Käthe, Anna and Gretchen Jensen. The photograph dates to the period 1903–5.

husband gone to eternity, and I was thrown on the mercy and help of the Lord alone'. At the time of his death Hans owned two elderly horses, an old wagon and eight oxen, a feather bed, a table, four chairs, a chest, some household utensils and tools, and an old gun.[139] These modest possessions were sold for 640 Rixdollars, and Emilie went to live with her daughter and son-in-law. The Koen family later moved to Haarlem [the site of a new mission village in the Langkloof], where Piet Koen bought some building lots and became deacon over the people, 'till it pleased the Lord to send us a missionary of the Berlin Society'. He died there in October 1862, leaving Christine penniless with ten minor children to support, but according to Emilie, the Lord did not forsake them.[140] At the time of her interview the children had all grown up, and Christine was nursing her old mother, 'till the Lord shall call me from this earth to heavenly bliss'.

Two instalments of Emilie's reminiscences appeared in the *Christian Express* in 1876. The second article mentioned that her young grandson

Niklaas Koen had just returned from Berlin after completing his theological studies. Niklaas, the seventh of Christine's large brood, had been more or less adopted by Haarlem's first German missionary, the Revd. F Prietsch, and his wife. The couple, who were childless, hoped that the studious lad would become a teacher. At about this time a well-wisher in Germany, Frau von Kocher, offered to sponsor a promising scholar who wanted to become a missionary, and Niklaas Koen was chosen. He left the Langkloof for Berlin in 1868 and returned, fully qualified, in 1875. He was the first South African of colour to complete such training in Germany. The Berlin Missionary Society sent him to work among the Venda people, and his fiancée came from Germany to marry him in 1878. Weakened by malaria, Niklaas died five years later at the age of thirty-one, leaving his widow Maria with two small children. His little son (who was Emilie's great-grandson) grew up to become the widely respected South African missionary Gerhard August Peter Kuhn (1881 to 1950).

Those who study Cape slavery find that their source material consists mainly of official documents or accounts by slave owners and travellers. Emilie Lehn's testimony covers a number of important aspects of the slave experience, and we are fortunate that someone sympathetic – probably Niklaas Koen – took the trouble to write down what she had to say.

Steyntje's search for justice

The best-known legal case in which a Cape slave family obtained their freedom is that of Emilie Lehn's older half sister, Steyntje, and her children.[141] It involved hearings in three separate courts, two at the Cape and one in Britain, over a period of seven years. Steyntje claimed her freedom on the grounds that she had cohabited with two of her previous masters, and had borne their children. In terms of a 1772 Resolution of the Court of India, which was ignored at the Cape, she should have been manumitted after the death of the master who had fathered her first child.

Steyntje was the daughter of Lea, slave of Johan Georg Stadler, and an unidentified German father who died within a few years of her birth. Lea, who was a teenage house slave when Steyntje was born in about 1777, became Stadler's housekeeper after his wife died in February 1785. Emilie recalled: 'From that time all the cares of the household fell upon the shoulders of my mother; all keys, and even the younger children were entrusted to her. The slaves knew why their master did not marry again and thanked him for it.'

This cryptic remark, which hints that Stadler was sexually involved with Lea, suggests that his domestic slaves preferred to work under the direction of an amenable slave housekeeper rather than a demanding white mistress. Be that as it may, in about 1792 Stadler (60) forced Lea's daughter Steyntje (15) to have 'carnal conversation' with him, and also ravished her sister Pamela from time to time. Both girls were unwilling, but they were his property and this gave him access to their bodies. Seven-year-old Emilie repressed the memory of their misery, and in her reminiscences she described Stadler as 'a pious and faithful man, who did good to us and treated us kindly in his house as long as he lived.'

When Steyntje eventually petitioned the court for her freedom, she alleged that she had refused his advances until he not only threatened to beat her, but actually flogged her, and witnesses reported that she and Pamela were sometimes dragged from their beds at night and forced to sleep with him under duress. As a result of this sexual abuse, Steyntje bore Stadler a son named Jacob in 1799. Stadler, who was prone to bouts of exaggerated penitence and piety, promised in the presence of his brother-in-law Jan Haussamer, that she and Jacob (alias Japie) would be emancipated after his death. It is worth noting that Stadler's relationship with his slave seems to have been accepted by the white community – and even by his late wife's brother – without comment or censure.

Unfortunately for Steyntje, Stadler broke his word. When he died in 1800, she discovered that he had neglected to make a will. She informed the Orphan Chamber of his pledge and suggested that certain supporting documents had been overlooked, but she did not persist with her claim for fear of punishment. All Stadler's slaves were publicly sold, and Steyntje was purchased by another elderly German, Johan Hendrik Weeber, who was separated from his second wife. Steyntje protested, knowing that Weeber had a reputation for ill-treating his slaves, but when Stadler's children offered to take her back, Weeber declared that, being unable to remarry, he had purchased her as his bed companion, and promised to emancipate her from slavery. Hearing this, Steyntje withdrew her objection and consented to his proposal, thinking that it would be to her advantage.

Weeber had previously manumitted one slave (his first wife), so Steyntje had reason to be hopeful. During the next three years they lived openly together, and she was regarded as the mistress of the house. Their friend Hendrik Nicolaas Bandel later testified that they dined, slept and walked together, like any married couple. Steyntje was always 'burgherly dressed', and Weeber repeatedly asserted that she was his wife and that Christina, the infant she was nursing, was his child. This was all very well, but Weeber was in financial difficulties and Steyntje could not compel him to keep his promise. In 1803 his assets, including Steyntje and her two children, were taken over by the Board of Insolvent Estates and sold for the benefit of his creditors. Weeber tried to argue that she and Christina should not be considered slaves, but the creditors saw things differently, and in January 1804 they were sold to Carel Wilhelm Dieleman for 1 390 Rixdollars. This forced separation is reported to have driven Weeber to drink.

Dieleman, a German merchant, had married his second wife, Adriana Berrangé, in 1801. Adriana produced two sons in quick succession and needed domestic help, so Steyntje lost the privileged status her sexual compliance had gained her and became a household drudge for the next eight years. She does not seem to have cohabited with Dieleman, and the fathers of her younger children, Fytje and Willem, have not been identified. Dieleman died in 1812, leaving an extensive estate that included Steyntje and her four children, who were valued at 6 000 Rixdollars. Adriana did not remain a widow for long. In April 1813, when she was 44, she married a Scottish bachelor named George Anderson (1769 to 1845), who had arrived at the Cape in 1799 as a clerk to Isaac Strombom, a Swedish merchant.

Anderson subsequently established his own business, but he does not seem to have been particularly prosperous. He moved into Dieleman's house at 49 Long Street after his marriage, and became Steyntje's *de facto* master. In the normal course of events, Anderson would have obtained complete control of his wife's property, but he was obliged by the terms of Dieleman's will to marry Adriana out of community of property. Most of the houses, stores and slaves attributed to Anderson in the *'opgaafs'* (tax returns) after 1814 were held by Adriana on behalf of her teenage sons. She was entitled to the revenues that accrued during their minority, but nothing more.

It was at this stage that Steyntje infuriated Anderson by deciding to test her claim to freedom. JG Stadler, Jacob's father, had been dead for 15 years, and JH Weeber, Christina's father, had died in 1808, so what made her do it? She may have been encouraged by a shadowy group of abolitionists who were keen to test the existing slave regulations in court. Several similar suits were already in process (including the one brought on behalf of Francina that featured in Chapter Six). Anderson's advocate later complained of 'a set of men, who either from interest, malice, or some other secret design, have used every means and every art to kindle the desire, and foster the hope of emancipation among the slaves of the colony'. Although these prior cases were ultimately unsuccessful, some appeals were still pending when Steyntje applied for an advocate to act as her curator.

Steyntje's suit is particularly interesting because her antagonist was a British subject. George Anderson, an aggressive, grasping man who was prone to exaggeration, opposed her 'pretended' claim on his wife's behalf. He behaved throughout as though he were her lawful owner, and his dogged attempts to retain her in slavery resulted in an expensive and humiliating defeat. In 1815 her advocate, MA Smuts, began the lengthy process of collecting affidavits to prove that she had been the concubine of both Stadler and Weeber, and had borne their children. While the case was pending, Steyntje was allowed to live out and pay Anderson the monthly fee commonly known as *'koeliegeld'*, from her earnings.

In September 1818, the conservative Court of Justice rejected Steyntje's application, but Smuts was granted leave to appeal on the grounds that she had suffered a miscarriage of justice. The opposing lawyer, Advocate JA Joubert, protested that her evidence was too 'trifling and insufficient' to warrant another hearing, and argued that Anderson had been deprived of her labour for a great length of time, and had been obliged to follow her to court and pay his own legal expenses, 'whilst his slave is vexing him *pro deo*'.[142] Joubert had more unpleasant things to say about Steyntje and her witnesses when the Court of Appeals, headed by the governor, sat in May 1819. Surprisingly, Lord Charles Somerset reversed the decision of the lower court, and in June Steyntje and her offspring were pronounced free persons.

Two weeks later Anderson petitioned for leave to appeal to the King in Council in London, Britain's highest court. He demanded that Steyntje and her children be re-assigned to him, and asked that her attorney be ordered to pay costs and damages. To Steyntje's dismay, Thomas Rowles, secretary to the Court of Appeals, ordered her to rejoin Anderson's household pending the outcome of his appeal. She believed that Rowles had done this at the insistence of Major Matthew Blake, the adjutant general, who wanted to take her daughter Christina into service, and she asked Acting Governor Donkin for redress, carefully signing her petition 'St[eyntje] Smit'.[143]

'This act of Mr Rowles I consider very oppressive and cruel; he knows I am too poor to live in Cape Town. I was unable to pay my rent, which caused me to reside in the country for cheapness.' She hinted that Blake had discreditable motives with regard to Christina, who had 'an invincible repugnance' to his service. Blake had threatened to lodge the family in the Tronk if Christina persisted in her refusal, and she was apprehensive of the outcome.

Steyntje's boldness in challenging the honour of a senior military officer may perhaps be attributed to an extraordinary circumstance – the patronage of Lord Charles Somerset, who was then on leave in Britain. She told Donkin that Somerset had been graciously pleased to deliver her papers to his own solicitors, who would act on her behalf in England. Somerset's partiality is confirmed in a letter he forwarded to the Earl of Bathurst in April 1820, requesting that Steyntje's case – 'as clear and just an one as ever was presented for judgment' – be carried to King in Council without expense to her.[144] And in July 1821, shortly before he left London, Somerset was at pains to inquire about the progress of the appeal.[145] After noting that Steyntje and her children were most anxious about the outcome, he stated that he would gladly be the bearer of their freedom on his return to the Cape. According to Somerset's detractors, his stormy governorship was characterised by extravagance, incompetence and a haughty and authoritarian disposition, but his sympathy for Steyntje, a harassed middle-aged slave, seems to indicate that a hitherto unsuspected streak of kindliness lurked beneath his prickly exterior.

The Cape Court of Appeals eventually directed that she and her children remain at large pending Anderson's appeal, but they were ordered to present themselves at court on the first day of each month. Major Blake got his way, however, and in June 1820 he reported that 'the girl Christina, daughter of Steintje [sic], is in my service'. He asked that Christina be excused further court attendance while she was under his protection.[146]

When the august legal body eventually met to discuss Steyntje's case, her conduct came in for much unfavourable comment. She was described as being a libidinous slave who had capriciously endangered the peace of every family by injuring the memory of her deceased master by the vilest accusations, which were supported only by the evidence of other 'objects of the stamp and class with herself' – her fellow slaves. Fortunately for Steyntje, her supporters were in the majority, and in June 1822 Lord Amhurst informed Somerset that the King in Council had confirmed her freedom.[147]

And so, after a seven-year legal battle, Steyntje and her children became free persons. However, in terms of the judgment, their names could not be erased from the Slave Register until they complied with the usual regulations, which included a payment of 200 Rixdollars to the poor fund of the Reformed Church. This was a large sum for an impoverished family to raise, and in 1823 Steyntje applied for exemption on the grounds that this requirement prejudiced her freedom, obtained by law in special circumstances.[148] But by then Somerset's patronage had reached its limits,

15. Cape Town in about 1785 to 1790, when Steyntje was a girl. The numerous flags indicate that it was still a Dutch mercantile outstation. The unidentified artist has managed to include (from L to R) the Castle and adjacent jetty, Rust en Vreugd, built in 1777 at the top of Buitenkant, the incomplete new hospital (used as a barracks from 1781), the Parade, the Groote Kerk, the Slave Lodge, the Tronk, the Lutheran Church and various warehouses, stores and batteries along the shore.

and her petition is endorsed: 'His Excellency has no authority for rescinding the decision of the High Court of Appeals in this case.'[149]

Steyntje's lengthy quest for justice must have been emotionally draining. Anderson's legal representatives demolished her reputation in court, and at least one of her witnesses betrayed her. She had to pay for the privilege of 'living out' during the seven-year judicial process, and at one stage she withdrew to the country because she could not afford to live in town. She had the added strain of two pregnancies during this stressful period, followed by the sorrow of losing her sons George and Jan in infancy. Anderson tried to detain her elder son Japie illegally, and her daughter Christina was forced to enter the service of Major Blake against her will, probably for financial reasons.

In 1827, a local printer named George Greig published a pamphlet entitled *Papers relating to the Manumission of Steyntje and her Children* to garner support for the abolitionist cause, but her case did not set a precedent. Sexual abuse of female domestic slaves by their owners appears to have been widespread, but most victims were too afraid to speak out, and the few who pressed their claims had as little success as Francina. Although Greig's pamphlet provides useful information about Steyntje's life in bondage, nothing is known about her after she became a free person at the age of 45. Her sister Pamela, who had also been sexually abused and apparently impregnated by Stadler, remained with his heirs until her death in April 1828.[150] Two of her closest relatives, her mother and her sister Emilie, had previously been sold away from Cape Town, and she may never have seen them again.

Surviving archival documents suggest that her adversary George Anderson was frequently at odds with his wife Adriana, his stepchildren, his slaves and the community at large. Although Adriana owned 11 properties, 3 stores, a piece of building ground and 22 slaves at the time of their marriage, the estate, valued at more than 83 000 Rixdollars, was intended for her sons procreated with Dieleman when they reached the age of 25. Meanwhile, she was bound to bring up and support them from the proceeds of their inheritance.

Dieleman's will had stipulated that, should she remarry, she was to retain control of her assets by means of an ante-nuptial contract. Such contracts were not legal in Britain, and Anderson seems to have had no scruples about taking charge of her affairs. He believed that he was entitled to compensation because Dieleman had purchased Steyntje in good faith in 1804. He drew up a grossly inflated statement of the losses his family had suffered as a result of Steyntje's suits, and in September 1823 he sent the colonial government a bill for more than 35 000 Rixdollars. This included a claim for 20 000 Rixdollars for Steyntje and her children (slaves who had been valued at 6 000 Rixdollars a decade earlier), and 9 600 Rixdollars for loss of earnings because he had been unable to hire them out for eight years. This preposterous demand was unsuccessful, and his attempt to negotiate a lesser settlement was pointedly ignored.

Anderson then tried to deduct various sums from his stepsons' inheritance. This prevented Anthony and Carel Christoffel Dieleman from receiving their paternal legacies when they fell due, and the young men eventually had to sue their mother for payment.[151] While they were prepared to bear the loss of the five slaves at their original value, they did not feel obliged to defray unnecessary legal expenses, and they totally rejected Anderson's other questionable claims. Adriana's death in 1834 precipitated a new round of legal wrangling. Anderson claimed almost £1 500 from his wife's insolvent estate – all the expenses he had tried to extort from his stepsons, plus some new ones.[152] When the decision went against him, he appealed, apparently without success.

George Anderson died in 1845 at the age of 76, seemingly a lonely and embittered old man.[153] His personal possessions – a stretcher with a straw mattress, blanket and pillow, and a few items of clothing – realised little more than £2 when auctioned.[154]

Ten

Tampering with the system

THE MAJORITY OF CAPE slave owners had no scruples about exercising absolute control over their slaves, fearing that any loss of power would place white lives at risk. In the worst days of slavery, they were permitted to administer punishment as they thought fit. Although some were excessively brutal, others stopped short of sadism in order to avoid incapacitating or killing valuable workers – incidents that might affect their good standing in the community. Many burgher families were related by marriage, and there was much visiting to and fro, so gossip and censure were best avoided. Nevertheless, farmers routinely inflicted severe 'domestic corrections' on their slaves for trivial offences, often forcing fellow slaves to hold the victim down while they plied the whip. Urban owners preferred to maintain control by psychological rather than physical abuse, usually by threatening to sell troublesome slaves upcountry if they misbehaved.

Maltreated slaves could complain to the fiscal, but their grievances were seldom treated seriously. Male slaves who had no taste for open resistance tried to devise coping mechanisms that minimised the amount of abuse they received and allowed them some sense of personal dignity. This was easier in the Cape district, where they were sometimes allowed to live out, and where they mingled with free persons of colour away from the prying eyes of their masters. Farm slaves were expected to be excessively obsequious and were sometimes forced to undertake degrading tasks like washing their owners' feet in public. Female slaves, who generally lived on intimate terms with their owners' families, tended to adopt attitudes of subservience and resignation as a means of self-protection. They worked under the direct supervision of their mistresses, and even minor expressions of frustration, like muttering, sighing, banging doors or pretending not to hear, were regarded as threats to domestic order.

The last decades of slavery were marked by incremental attempts by the British authorities to improve the lot of slaves and moderate the power of their masters. In 1816, compulsory registration of slaves was introduced and an office was established to compile the necessary records. Dozens of large leather-bound registers containing particulars of thousands of slaves have been preserved in the Cape Town Archives Repository. Every slave owner was listed separately, and space was provided for the name, gender, age, origin, occupation and status of each of his slaves. Clerks inscribed these details in beautiful copper-plate script, and all subsequent births, deaths, desertions, manumissions, transfers, inheritances or special conditions were entered in the appropriate columns. Penalties and fines were imposed for neglecting to inform the authorities of any changes, and hundreds of appeals were received during the next 18 years from defaulting owners claiming to have been entirely ignorant of their responsibilities and begging for relief. Governors were usually sympathetic, and most fines were drastically reduced.

Further measures were introduced in 1823, 1826, 1830 and 1831. Among other regulations, the flogging of female slaves was restricted and then prohibited, and limits were placed on the number of strokes a male slave could receive. The new laws were difficult to enforce, but prosecutions became more common towards the end of the 1820s, when landdrosts were replaced by magistrates. These changes – and rumours of possible emancipation – astounded many slave owners, and there were widespread protests, particulary in 1830 when the vexed question of presenting punishment record books for inspection arose. Stellenbosch slave owners caused such a disturbance that the regulation was quietly overlooked, and open hostility gradually subsided into a nagging sense of discontent.

Complaints by slaves of excessive or unwarranted punishment were usually investigated, and although there were relatively few convictions, owners sometimes had to travel long distances to explain themselves. They faced a minimum fine of £10 if found guilty – a considerable sum in those days. The slave grapevine seems to have operated very efficiently, and rural slaves were surprisingly well informed about their new rights, in sharp contrast to their masters, who claimed to be entirely unaware of the unwelcome proclamations, citing their complete isolation on their farms as the reason for their ignorance.

Documents in the Cape Town Archives Repository show that flogging was common for minor infringements like impertinence, slovenliness, disregarding orders, neglecting their work, breaking things or quarrelling. Josephine was chastised for not reporting she had finished her needlework; Adam for giving an insolent answer to his master's son; Onverwagt for not ploughing properly with a defective plough; and Roos for her aggravating tongue.[155] Betje was flogged for not being faithful to her so-called 'husband', and so was Roset for being careless and slovenly.[156] Saul's tooth was loosened in one assault and he was beaten again for daring to complain.[157] Fortuin was lashed for waiting until daybreak before slaughtering an ox, because he could not see in the dark.[158] Aploon was punished for not making an egg sauce, as was twelve-year-old Dina, for neglecting her duty and making her clothes into dolls' dresses.[159] More serious misconduct included minor pilfering, temporary desertion, losing livestock or making false complaints.

Not all slaves were flogged. Some were put in stocks or fetters and others were kicked, slapped or punched, or had their hair pulled. Lydia was struck on the head with an iron ladle, and another Dina was hit with a jug and dowsed with water.[160] January, aged 15, who ran off to visit his mother, was tied by the neck and forced to keep pace with his master's horse for two hours.[161]

Slaves were required to substantiate their complaints with physical evidence (bruises, contusions, lacerated flesh or other injuries) or corroborating testimony by credible witnesses. However, many fellow slaves were chary of speaking out for fear of victimisation, and complainants who were dismissed for lack of evidence were often punished for making false accusations. Wounds spoke more loudly than words, but there were sometimes long delays before a medical examination took place, during which time some healing occurred. In 1834, Dr Daniel O'Flinn, district surgeon of Stellenbosch, reported that local burghers were so antagonistic towards him for carrying out his duty towards abused slaves that his private practice was in serious decline.[162]

Insolence was regarded as particularly aggravating. In 1830, Pieter de Villiers of Paarl, the young son of a widow, was convicted for illegally beating Theresia twice within 24 hours for using injurious language.[163] His mother, who tried unsuccessfully to have his fine withdrawn, described him as a dutiful son who had acted to protect her and deter other slaves from following Theresia's bad example. And when Alie, slave of TD du Plessis of Uitenhage, protested about a punishment inflicted on his child, he received 25 lashes for daring to complain with his hat on.[164]

Many convicted burghers hurried to the notary to draft a plea for mitigation, invariably citing provocation, ignorance of the law, poverty and a large and needy family as reasons why the governor should reduce their fines. Most of these petitions came from the outlying agricultural districts, where relations between master and slave were frequently characterised by extreme brutality. Urban slaves had ready access to the Slave Office, and their owners generally made use of more sophisticated and less violent methods of control.

Fines were sometimes reduced, depending on the recommendation of local Slave Protectors, some of whom had remarkably little sympathy for their charges. After a series of inconsistent decisions, Colonel Bell, the colonial secretary, recommended that owners who had paid admission-of-guilt fines should not be granted refunds because no evidence had been led in court. Very occasionally, slaves who were victims of deliberate cruelty were confiscated by the Crown. Bell, who advised a succession of governors, found the petitions irritating, but he generally consulted the magistrates who had heard the cases before taking a firm position. Some officials were only too ready to recommend leniency, based on little more than the owner's reputed benevolence and lack of previous convictions, while others

16. Imaginary depiction of a common scene. This image was engraved in London in 1802 and published in an abridged edition of John Barrow's Travels into the interior of Southern Africa. *Although the palm trunk and other minor details are incorrect, numerous Cape slaves were tied to trees or whipping posts and punished by* knegts *[overseers] in the presence of their owners.*

stood by their decisions to sentence tyrannical owners on the sometimes uncorroborated testimony of their victims. Such contradictions were inevitable – slavery was an evil and outmoded system which no amount of tampering could improve.

Deborah of the Cape

In April 1832, Cornelis van der Watt requested a reduction of the £10 fine imposed by Mr Aspeling, the resident magistrate of Swellendam for illegally punishing Deborah (20), his only slave.[165] He declared that she had conducted herself 'so much improperly and insolently' that his wife, being ignorant of the law, had inflicted 'a few stripes on the body' as a correction.

After his petition had been forwarded to Aspeling for comment, a far more dramatic and damning story came to light. On 15 February 1832, Deborah was instructed to churn the milk for butter. As was her custom, she placed a cloth round the top of the churn to prevent the contents from splashing. Seeing this, her mistress flew into a rage and inflicted 'about six stokes with a switch or thin rattan' on her shoulders. She believed that the cloth had previously been applied to an ulcerated breast as a poultice, 'of which circumstance it would seem that Deborah was ignorant, as the cloth was clean washed when she put it on'.

Although this was an illegal punishment, Van der Watt was not prosecuted for his wife's transgression but for assaulting Deborah the very next day 'by striking her several blows with a stick until it broke, and then beating her with an ox-riem over the arms, back and thighs'. Van der Watt denied this and pleaded not guilty, but he was convicted 'on the single evidence of the complainant, on whose posterior and left side four marks ... of recent laceration of the skin were found,' and whose testimony the magistrate saw no reason to doubt. The cause of the beating was her failure to provide wood for the oven, but it appeared that Deborah had not been allowed sufficient time to go and collect it. Aspeling concluded: 'It must also be remarked that the beating was inflicted when [the] complainant was about six months gone with child. All which circumstances considered, I cannot take it upon myself to recommend [the] memorialist to His Excellency's clemency.'

The fact that Deborah had been beaten while pregnant outraged Colonel Bell, who had previously scribbled caustic comments in the margins of Van der Watt's ingenuous petition, including: 'Is this in any degree possible?', when the farmer asserted that his wife was ignorant of the law. 'I give it as my opinion that this man has got off too easily,' he wrote, and suggested that the case ought to have been transferred to the Circuit Court for trial before a judge. After interviews with the attorney general and the Protector of Slaves, Bell allowed himself to be persuaded that justice had indeed been done, and Van der Watt was informed that the fine would not be mitigated. Three months after her maltreatment, Deborah gave birth to Van der Watt's second slave, a boy named Jephta.[166]

Saartje of the Cape

In 1834, a widow named Ester Maria le Roux (1793 to 1862) of the farm Cabrière in the Franschhoek valley was sent to prison in Stellenbosch for illegally assaulting Saartje of the Cape, her housemaid's young daughter. Saartje had been born in Stellenbosch in 1823, but in 1826 she and her mother Sara were sold to Abraham Josua le Roux for 1 600 Rixdollars. He didn't have the funds to pay for his purchase and a bond was issued that his widow had not redeemed in 1833.

By the time she was ten, Saartje worked alongside her mother in the house and had little time to play with her younger brother Adolph and baby sister Theresie.[167] By the summer of 1833, the physical abuse of female slaves had been officially outlawed at the Cape for several years, but when Saartje returned home one Saturday afternoon after being absent without leave, her mistress was so angry that she felled the child with a blow to the cheek. When Saartje still refused to answer any questions, she was sent to a back room to await further retribution.

Sara, who had been washing clothes in the yard, followed anxiously. She told the widow that her heart was very sore, and asked to be present at the punishment, but she was given a slap in the face and told to return to her work. By then, Ester Maria's temper was dangerously out of control, as Sara afterwards found to her detriment. 'I mixed starch in the kitchen, and on giving my mistress the spoon with which I had done it, she was angry with me for having used it, and laying hold of me by the hair, beat me on the head and face so that my mouth bled and I fell down.'

When Sara went into the hall later to iron, she was horrified to see Saartje sitting on her haunches in a little store-room off the main bedroom, stark naked. Sara knew that the clay floor was infested with red ants that Ester Maria had been unable to eradicate, despite frequently pouring boiling water into their holes. 'On seeing the child there, I asked my mistress if it was right, after having punished her, to put her naked in that place. She said she would do it, and she would shew [her] to every person who came to that place.'

The child was still there when the widow shut the bedroom door firmly and went to bed, and Sara did not see her daughter again until Sunday morning, when she came home from having driven the cattle out and fetched some firewood. Saartje was sweeping out the bedroom, and her mother was unable to speak to her until later, when she saw her coming out of the stable, walking stiffly and weeping. She said her feet hurt, but it was not until their mistress went out in the afternoon that Sara examined her and found sores between her toes and fingers, some with ants still attached.

She also saw fresh wounds and other marks of a severe flogging on the child's loins, buttocks and thighs, but what really grieved her was the news that after administering the illegal punishment, Ester Maria had sent her daughter Leentje to the kitchen for the skimmer, a large flat perforated spoon, which she used to scoop up some of the ants and throw them over Saartje's body. Her hair was so full of ants next day that Sara was obliged to cut it off, a cruel blow as most female slaves were proud of their tresses, and shorn heads were regarded as a particular indignity.

Sara herself was ill-clothed and had previously laid two complaints against her mistress for physical abuse, but they had been rejected for lack of evidence. Three weeks previously she had been beaten so severely with a wagon trace that it tore her husband Ezau's old jacket, which she was wearing at the time. She had wanted to complain again, but had been dissuaded by Ezau, one of the widow's three field slaves, because she had no witnesses – Ester Maria had made sure that the door was closed before she broke the law. The brutal attack on her daughter was the final straw. Sara's indignation gave her the courage to defy her mistress and walk the twenty miles to Stellenbosch to lay a complaint with the Assistant Protector of Slaves. Her testimony reads: 'On Sunday afternoon I left the farm with my children, to come and complain, as I cannot any longer bear the continued ill-treatment which my mistress inflicts on me.'[168]

Dr O'Flinn, the district surgeon, examined Saartje after her arrival and provided a damning report. She had a contusion on her left cheek, and the skin on her loins and thighs had been extensively broken by heavy blows from a doubled flexible instrument. He believed that the wounds between her fingers might indeed have been caused by ant bites. Mr Dickinson, the Assistant Protector of Slaves and clerk of the peace, issued a warrant of apprehension, and the widow Le Roux duly appeared before him. When her slaves' statements were read to her, she made a general denial, and her daughter Leentje dismissed Saartje's complaint about the skimmer.

The case was set down for trial at the next Circuit Court, and in the meantime Dickinson sent Saartje, the principal witness, to the slave school in the village, in order to have her instructed in the nature of the oath she would be required to take. Her mother Sara had lived in Stellenbosch prior to being sold to the Le Rouxs, and bore a very good character. This singled her out as being worthy of assistance – in those days, compassion was seldom expended on those regarded as undeserving. In view of the widow's 'embittered feelings', Dickinson allowed Sara to work for her keep prior to the trial, and she was supplied with the much-needed clothing that her mistress had neglected to provide.

Housekeeping was a laborious business in the 1830s, and Ester Maria was extremely annoyed when her case was postponed to the second Circuit. In March 1834, she complained to the new governor, Sir Benjamin D'Urban, giving him her version of events and informing him that she had satisfied the Assistant Protector that all the 'unfounded and absurd charges' against her were false. She alleged that she had merely inflicted three stripes on Saartje with a little whip belonging to one of her children. Unfortunately Dickinson had not returned her slaves, and their services would now be lost to her for eight months. She believed they should work, 'instead of idling their time in indolence or vice at Stellenbosch, or being employed by others'.

D'Urban forwarded her letter to Dickinson, who denied that he was satisfied that the slaves' complaints were false. He said that he had agreed to return them to their mistress, provided her brother-in-law stood surety that she would abstain from further beatings, but this offer had not been accepted. Her petition was therefore refused.

And so Sara and her three children remained in Stellenbosch until July 1834, when the chief justice, Sir John Wylde, and his entourage, descended on the village. Unfortunately Saartje's spell at school had not taught her the difference between heaven and hell, and she was found incompetent to testify. This meant that the widow's advocate, Mr van Ryneveld, was denied the opportunity of trying to expose the child as an untrustworthy witness during cross-examination. Realising the damaging nature of the surgeon's report, he offered to plead guilty on his client's behalf, provided all references to the red ants and the skimmer were withdrawn from the indictment.

The charge against the widow was hastily amended to one of assaulting Saartje by beating her with a whip and her fists, and confining her without clothes in a pantry. No further inquiry was needed, and the jury confirmed her guilt.[169] Wylde imposed the customary £10 fine and added two further penalties. He ordered Saartje to be confiscated to the Crown, and he condemned the widow, who was the mother of five minor children, to a month in the Stellenbosch gaol.

Ester Maria's plea for the mitigation of this unusually stiff sentence reached the Colonial Office within days.[170] She claimed to have no one to look after her farm or her children, and begged His Excellency to recognise her deplorable situation and remit her imprisonment, but D'Urban saw no cause for clemency in a case that appeared to him to have been one of 'very aggravating cruelty'. Meanwhile, the trial was reported in the press and caused a good deal of dissatisfaction. An anonymous juryman, one of nine local burghers who heard the case, protested that there had been serious irregularities in the court proceedings, and publicised the fact that Saartje, the chief witness, could not be called because she did not understand the implication of the oath required of her.[171]

Ester Maria duly went to prison in Stellenbosch, but the experience of being singled out for such a degrading punishment left her entirely unrepentant. She accused the jurors of incompetence and blamed her advocate, Mr van Ryneveld, for pleading guilty contrary to her wishes. In October 1834, she forwarded a rambling petition, based on dubious points of law, asking to have the other penalties remitted.[172] Saartje's mother, Sara, who had taken the child to Stellenbosch to complain to the Assistant Protector of Slaves, came in for the full force of the widow's wrath. She described Sara as a bad character who had complained unsuccessfully twice before, and used unfair means to try and rid herself of her mistress. As for Saartje, the widow knew of instances where slave girls had suffered fatal consequences while playing truant, and she had been punished for her own good. She could scarcely claim to have been severely flogged, when she had managed to walk the twenty English miles to Stellenbosch the very next day. Ester Maria declared that if she had perhaps exceeded the limits of lawful punishment, it was entirely due to the obstinacy and provocation of her ten-year-old slave, who would not answer her questions, and asked His Excellency to consider her imprisonment a sufficient punishment and remit the fine and Saartje's confiscation.

D'Urban consulted Major GJ Rogers, the Protector of Slaves, who replied: 'I do not find that Mrs Roux is deserving of any commiseration. Far from showing any contrition for the ferocity of her behaviour to her slave, she appears throughout to defend her right to do with her, what it pleased her to do. During her imprisonment, Mrs Roux appears not to have felt any sense of shame for the cause of her confinement, and as it is evident that the payment of the pecuniary fine and the confiscation of her slave has reached her heart, I should be sorry to learn that the only thing she seems capable of feeling should be removed.'

In rejecting her plea, D'Urban probably reinforced the sense of grievance felt by the conservative Dutch-speaking community at British attempts to introduce a new social order. They resented the regulations, introduced from 1823, which were intended to improve the lot of their slaves, believing that they undermined authority and encouraged indiscipline. They were offended by the notion that a Christian widow could be sent to gaol on the word of an uneducated slave girl. In 1843, the voortrekker Anna Steenkamp, niece of Piet Retief, ascribed the impetus for the Great Trek not only to 'the shameful and unjust proceedings with reference to the freedom of our slaves', but more particularly to their being placed on an equal footing with Christians, 'contrary to the laws of God and the natural distinction of race and colour, so that it was intolerable for any decent Christian to bow down beneath such a yoke'.[173]

According to the Register of Slave Appraisals for the Stellenbosch district drawn up after the general abolition of slavery in 1834, the widow Le Roux, one of four slave owners listed as residing at Cabrier [Cabrière] in Franschhoek, was entitled to compensation for five slaves: Dampie, Esau, Adolph, Sara and Theresie, so Saartje had indeed been confiscated.[174]

Arend and November of the Cape

Abraham Benjamin de Villiers (1785 to 1851), a wine farmer from 'behind the Paarl', was the great-grandson of Jacques de Villiers, one of three Huguenot brothers who founded the prolific De Villiers family at the Cape. He married three times and produced 13 children.[175] He ran his estate, Ruitevalley, with 22 adult slaves, mostly males born locally or in Mozambique.[176] Archival documents indicate that he was authoritarian, paternalistic, inconsistent and sometimes devious, and he did not scruple to use torture to extract confessions.

In April 1830, his coachman, Arend of the Cape (42), walked to Stellenbosch to report him for maltreatment. Although slaves had the right to complain, they were well aware of the risks they faced when they eventually returned to their irate owners. Some slaves were lodged in prison pending their hearings, but magistrates usually released those whose cases were set down for the next Circuit Court, considering it a hardship to confine them for up to six months. On 19 April, the resident magistrate of Stellenbosch informed the Assistant Guardian of Slaves that he had sent Arend home, adding: 'I am at a loss to decide any mode to be adopted in such cases, and I do not think that the Government can be charged with the [prison] expenses.'[177]

Arend's testimony, given in the Circuit Court in September 1830 and reported in the press, was remarkably succinct and unemotional.[178]

> On a Monday morning in April I went to Cape Town. Before we got into the wagon my mistress said: 'What smell of wine is this?' On the road my master was sitting by me; I was driving and he held the whip. My master said: 'What smell of wine is this?' I replied that I knew of no wine, that perhaps he might smell the medicine which I had been taking, having been sick for some days.
>
> On Wednesday at midnight we returned. Nothing was said more about the wine. On Friday morning I was sitting mending the harness. My master came up and said: 'Where did you get that drink from?' I said it was no wine but medicine that he smelt. He then said: 'No, you shall confess to me.' I said: 'Master, I do not know anything of it, I am innocent.' He then laid hold of my jacket, took me to the front of the harness room and told the young master fetch the ring-bolt, into which my master locked my hands and feet. Taking hold of the end of it, [he] threw me over on my side and kicked me in the mouth.

The unfortunate slave was entirely helpless, doubled up painfully with his hands between his feet. After sending his son to cut some quince twigs, De Villiers saddled his horse and rode away. Arend continued:

> I could not sit up. I therefore called old Moos [a basket-maker] who was in the harness room, who came and lifted me up so that I could sit up. I was in great pain across my loins from my body being bent down to my feet. When my master returned, which was in half an hour, he told his son that he had not brought twigs enough – he must go and fetch twenty. My master had the twigs cleaned and scorched in the fire.
>
> I was then taken out of the irons, and he called for some boys – Klaas, Esau, Africa, Elias, November, David and Moos – and I was ordered to undress. I was held over a wall, and my master flogged me with the quince twigs, with which I was punished by five at a time. I think I received about 25 or 26 [strokes], but the punishment was so great I could not tell how much. All the while I was being punished, my master said I must confess to him from where the smell of wine had come.
>
> On the same day after the punishment I ran away. I have been a slave of

> Mr de Villiers about ten years. The irons were on the place when I went there [and] I have seen them used there. My back was very sore from the flogging. My lips had been sore but were quite healed before I had the kick. The mark on my belly was caused by being held over the wall. I was not impertinent to my master when he taxed me with having been drinking wine – only said I was innocent.

Moos Alexander, Klaas and Esau all corroborated Arend's account. Moos described the slave's pain during his period in irons as being almost unbearable. Esau reported that he had held Arend's feet when he was laid across the wall, and added, significantly: 'I heard my master say that Arend had received 25 lashes, but I do not know what 25 is.'

When Dr O'Flinn, the district surgeon, examined Arend on 17 April 1830, he found severe livid contusions with the skin broken across the upper part of his back and shoulders. The injury to his mouth was also consistent with violence. Referring to the irons, which were displayed in court, he said: 'I am of the opinion that the ring-bolt applied in the manner described must have caused great pain and deprived [Arend] of all power of motion and of any way of assisting himself.'

Three cases of slave abuse were heard during the session, but two were thrown out.[179] Faced with incontrovertible evidence, the jury had no option but to find De Villiers guilty, but recommended him to mercy on account of the testimony given by several local officials, who claimed that he had a kind disposition, and the evidence of some of his own slaves. Mr Justice Kekewich imposed the usual £10 fine – not much of a hardship for a wealthy farmer – and assured De Villiers that he might return home without the slightest stigma attaching to his name from the result of the trial.[180] Despite this shameful partiality, news of Arend's moral victory would have heartened his fellow slaves, especially those who were too timid to complain.

During the next three years moves towards emancipation gathered momentum in London – far too quickly for the comfort of Cape farmers, who had been accustomed to owning their labour for more than 170 years. In December 1833, Major GJ Rogers, Protector of Slaves – a man who should have had slave interests at heart – prepared a confidential report about the attitude of slave owners in the western division towards the coming changes.[181]

He reported that that they were astounded at the speed with which matters had progressed, and could foresee no benefits, only humiliation and annoyance. They described the proposals as illegal, unjust and injudicious, and were filled with misgivings about losing the assistance they needed to support their families. Instead of a general emancipation, they had envisaged a gradual scheme in which infants became free after a certain number of years. Rogers agreed with their contention that some slaves were not fit for the boon of freedom and would never be any use either to themselves or the community.

Owners disliked the proposed period of apprenticeship (1834 to 1838) and complained of increasing impertinence and insubordination among their slaves, particularly females, who knew 'a thousand modes to vex and annoy'. They did not see how they would be able to control their labour if apprentices were allowed to complain to special magistrates, and if their right to administer 'domestic correction' was removed. They believed that their emancipated slaves would to flock to Cape Town, where the willing and industrious would find work, while the rest – idle and evil-minded – would form gangs to commit outrage, robbery, conflagration and even murder, venting their first outbursts on their former owners. Rogers agreed, and expressed sympathy for the 'very peculiar situation' facing slave owners. The best way to placate them would be to appraise their valuable slaves accurately for the purposes of compensation, and to appoint local lawmakers to frame acceptable regulations – 'overseas input will of necessity be disastrous.'

Much of this alarmist speculation proved to be inaccurate, but the mid-1830s were years of tension at the Cape, particularly in the farming districts. It was during this period that a violent confrontation took place on Ruitevalley involving November of the Cape – a witness to Arend's illegal punishment – and Jacob, eldest son of Abraham de Villiers.

One evening in March 1834, Arend complained to his master that November (25) had assaulted him whilst drunk. Jacob de Villiers ran after the intoxicated slave, whom he would have known since childhood, and collared him, but November lashed out and stabbed his pursuer under the left ear before running off. Jacob's father considered the wound to be 'of a very dangerous nature', and sent a message asking the district surgeon and the clerk of the peace at Stellenbosch to come and examine the victim and conduct an inquest. Much to De Villiers' indignation, these officials did not hurry to his farm. Instead, he was informed that he would have to pay if he required Dr O'Flinn's services. He was particularly aggrieved about this, and complained to the governor that the surgeon already drew a salary from the public treasury.[182]

Sir Benjamin D'Urban invited the clerk of the peace to explain. Mr Dickinson replied that if young De Villiers had been in any danger, he would have sent someone to inspect his injuries and take a statement. When he questioned the messenger, however, he was told that the knife had struck the jawbone and the victim was doing well. De Villiers, an opulent farmer residing within an hour's call of three private doctors, had not sent for them because they were unwilling to treat injuries that might require them to give evidence in court. Under these circumstances, Dickinson did not see why the district surgeon should attend without a fee. Fortunately no one had died, so there had been no need to conduct an inquest.

D'Urban forwarded the papers to the attorney general for a legal opinion. Sir Anthony Oliphant was not known for his energy, but his brief reply highlighted the weakness of De Villiers' argument: 'If Mr de Villiers thought the wound was of a serious nature, it was his duty to have caused it to be examined by a regularly admitted medical man – but if he did not think so, then it was not his duty to do so.' Needless to say, young Jacob soon recovered.

November returned to the farm voluntarily and was arrested.[183] The case was set down for trial at the next Circuit Court in July, but instead of leaving him to languish in the Stellenbosch gaol, De Villiers bailed him out, presumably to save prison fees and enjoy the benefit of his labour. Although the British had made themselves extremely unpopular by attempting to ameliorate slavery at the Cape, severe penalties were still in force for slaves who harmed their owners. November had been in court before for threatening violence, and he was sentenced to 75 lashes, followed by 48 hours in solitary confinement and two years' hard labour on the public works.[184] After suffering the first two penalties, he escaped from a work gang at Stellenbosch in August 1834 and disappeared. If recaptured, he could expect another trial and a longer prison sentence.

Some twenty months later De Villiers forwarded a remarkable petition to D'Urban expressing deep sympathy and concern for the slave who had attacked his son.[185] Wishing to reclaim November from his state of vagrancy and restore him to service, De Villiers asked that the rest of his sentence be remitted, 'so that when [he] may return or be apprehended, he may be free ...' He added that his slave had shown great contrition for his alcohol-induced crime, and declared that he and his son had cordially forgiven the offender. If pardoned, November would not only return, but would prove to be a good subject in future.

Colonel Bell, the acerbic colonial secretary, was so astonished that he called it 'the most extraordinary request I remember to have seen'. The governor was equally skeptical and suspected that the farmer knew where November was hiding. He wrote: 'If so, it is his duty to inform the authorities. Let him produce the deserter – then I will consider the application.'

There is no evidence that De Villiers complied. His solicitude was probably prompted by financial considerations. After the abolition of slavery in 1834, officials went from farm to farm appraising slaves for the purposes of compensation, which was funded by the British treasury. No compensation was payable for deserters, and the register shows that De Villiers stood to forfeit £75 for his missing slave.[186] Armed with a free pardon, he no doubt hoped to entice November back into service, but D'Urban was wise to such tricks.

Rebecca of the Cape

It should not be assumed that injustice towards slaves was limited to the Dutch settler community. Rebecca of the Cape, who later became a flamboyant street character in Cape Town, was distressed by the treatment she received during her service with an English family. She was born in the 1790s and appears from later photographs to have been of African descent. She survived until 1873, and it seems likely that her unstable behaviour was brought on by her experience of slavery.

She was first registered as a housemaid in the Stellenbosch district in 1816, one of 24 working slaves and nine slave children owned by Daniel Brink (1784 to 1840) of the farm Geduld at Eerste River.[187] Rebecca found a partner on the farm and gave birth to four sons during the next nine years: Manuel, April, Bastiaan and Soldaat. Brink's wife Elizabeth could call upon the services of seven housemaids and a cook, and during the 1820s she hired Rebecca out in Cape Town. Just how an inexperienced young English couple came to employ this Dutch-speaking country slave is an intriguing question that has yet to be answered.

Rebecca joined the Revd. Fearon Fallows (1789 to 1831) and his wife Mary Anne in about 1825, together with her infant son Soldaat, while her other boys stayed behind on the farm. Fallows, the son of a Cumberland weaver, was a brilliant mathematician who managed to obtain sufficient patronage to study at Cambridge, where he was later ordained.[188] In August 1821, he became the first British astronomer to serve at the Cape, and he occupied rented accommodation in Cape Town while his new observatory was under construction on a barren eminence near the Black River.

Fallows hoped that his new appointment would mark the beginning of a successful and prosperous career, but his health was poor and he had not allowed for the high cost of living at the Cape, particularly with regard to house rent, food and servants. Slaves could not be hired for less than 25 Rixdollars a month, and required 'more looking after than they are worth'. He anticipated new difficulties when he moved to the Observatory in 1827, as free servants and hired slaves were reluctant to live in such an isolated situation.

By 1825 he seems to have concluded that the best way to solve his servant problem was to buy his own domestic slaves – a considerable financial outlay, given his precarious financial position. His first purchase, Charlotta, was just 13 years old.[189] The following year he decided to buy Rebecca and Soldaat from Daniel Brink, but he struck an unexpected snag. According to new legislation, a slave mother could not be sold apart from her offspring under the age of ten, but Fallows could not afford to buy and support four unproductive children. He seems to have prevailed upon Rebecca to forego her rights in terms of her three eldest boys, in return for the prospect of possible emancipation.

In September 1826, the Guardian of Slaves petitioned the Court of Justice to allow the sale to go through because 'the mother represented ... that she had been living for some time in the family of the Revd. Mr Fallows, and that he was anxious to purchase herself and her youngest child, and as she was pleased with her situation and had hopes that if Mr and Mrs Fallows returned to England they might take her with them, she preferred leaving her other children with Mr Brink, by whom she was certain they would be well treated, and with whom their father resided'.[190]

The Court raised no objections, and Rebecca and Soldaat were duly transferred to Fallows, who took it upon himself to baptise the child under the name 'James Robert Soldaat' at the Observatory in October

1826 – presumably his temporary observatory at Zorg-en-Lust, a site now occupied by the Ladies' Christian Home. It seems unlikely that Rebecca would have managed to maintain contact with her little sons on the farm, and this painful separation may have marked the beginning of her mental instability.

Fallows' attitude to slaves and apprentices was probably coloured by his own struggle to rise above his circumstances. He wished to improve their lives, but it was up to them to seize the limited opportunities he offered. In return, he expected absolute loyalty and obedience. In 1827, he and his wife Mary Anne moved into the astronomer's fine new residence in a wing of the remote new Observatory. The building lacked servants' quarters, and Charlotta, Rebecca and Soldaat are presumed to have slept in the underground cellars.

Fallows died in July 1831, aged 42, weakened by worry and disappointment. He was buried in the grounds of the Observatory, and his childless widow prepared to return to England. Before she left, Mrs Fallows manumitted Charlotta and her baby Fanny, but whatever promises had been made to Rebecca were forgotten, and she and Soldaat were sold to William Dickson on behalf of his five minor children.[191] Less than a year later they were sold again, this time to John Carter for the benefit of his infant son Rowland.[192] Rebecca seems to have remained at the Observatory as a hired slave and was later sketched there by another British astronomer, CP Smyth.[193]

She suppressed her disappointment prior to the abolition of slavery in December 1834, but when she discovered that she was to be apprenticed without pay for a further four years, she petitioned the governor, Sir Benjamin D'Urban, protesting that she had already arranged to purchase herself in instalments from Brink for 800 Rixdollars, when Fallows 'was kindly pleased to pay [the sum] in two instalments and agreed ... that she should serve him until the money was paid back'.[194]

Fallows allegedly told her that he was not allowed to have any slaves, and she could therefore consider herself a free person. She had consented to be sold without three of her children, then all under the age allowed by law for separation, because she thought it was best for her welfare. D'Urban forwarded Rebecca's petition to Major GJ Rogers, the ex-Protector of Slaves, who dismissed it as a fabrication, and commented: 'Had she behaved well in the late Revd. Mr Fallows' service, I doubt not he would have been disposed to do everything kind as well for herself as her son, but for some time previous to [his] decease, Rebecca became so insubordinate, and so grossly misconducted herself, that his widow determined upon her sale, having the legal right to dispose of them as slaves'.

With his customary lack of sympathy for human frailty, Rogers concluded disapprovingly: 'Rebecca has lately given herself so much up to drinking that she is at times nearly brought in to a state of insanity from its effects.' Rebecca was informed that she had no claim to immediate freedom, and had to endure another four years of servitude before she embarked on her career as a symbol of underclass defiance.

17. 'Queen Rebecca', an ex-slave photographed in the 1860s. She once belonged to the Revd. Fearon Fallows, the British astronomer who oversaw the construction of what is now the South African Astronomical Observatory in the suburb of Observatory. She grew increasingly eccentric later in life and was well known as a 'street character' when she died in August 1873.

By 1843 she was a well-known 'street character', who claimed kinship with British royalty and greeted the respectable classes with annoying familiarity. She was often the butt of crude humour and unkind jibes. *De Verzamelaar* published a 'pretended family history of Lady Rebecca, alias Bekkie', describing her appearance and commenting that her temper, when provoked, was warm and vindictive.[195] In 1851, this 'poor deranged coloured woman, who for many years past has been a constant and noisy, though harmless, visitor at the public offices,' was arrested for abusing some ladies, 'who, being strangers in the place, were very much alarmed'.[196]

During her trial, 'Queen Rebecca' gravely produced a document scribbled over in red ink, which she declared was her defence, written by Sir Robert Peel (a noted British reformer). It availed her little, and she endured eight days in the Tronk on a diet of rice water, and was ordered to find bail for her good behaviour. When not accosting others, Rebecca talked to herself in a mixture of English and Dutch. She knew all the prominent people and would address them in 'very free and often uncomplimentary terms' when she met them in the streets during her midday walks. Those who mocked her, or failed to give her a coin or two, received a bitter tongue lashing.

She is said to have ornamented herself with ribbons, rags, flowers and feathers, but in at least one photograph she is neatly dressed in the fashions of the late 1850s, and appears to have a well-developed sense of style. Her passing in August 1873 was marked by brief obituaries in two leading city newspapers and a sentimental poem by WL Sammons. According to the *Standard and Mail*, Rebecca had long been a privileged beggar whose appeals could be forceful at times, but she would be missed by many. She was assisted in her last days by a few charitable people who thought well of her, despite her eccentric manners and language.[197] Sammons suggested that although she had a mercurial temperament and a sharp tongue, there was a fine line between reason and derangement. When she dropped her queenly airs, her words were quiet, natural and plain, and he wondered what had caused her eccentricity – 'her flaunty dress and flighty chat'. He speculated that she had been crossed in love when young, and he ended on a compassionate note by observing that frailty was a common human condition.[198] Sammons, a writer and editor who came to the Cape from Britain in 1843, would not have known of Rebecca's experiences as a slave.

Strangely enough, her delusions of grandeur were realised in an uncanny manner after her death, when her reputed daughter Martha married a down-at-heel Englishman who later became the eighth Earl of Stamford.

Eleven

The dawn of freedom

MOST OF THE PRESSURE to abolish slavery in the British Empire came from Britain, and although colonial officials at the Cape paid lip-service to these ideals, they were careful not to offend the influential slave-owning section of the population – a conflict of interests that prevented the formation of an official anti-slavery movement at the Cape. The only abolitionist organisation to receive government support was 'The Cape of Good Hope Philanthropic Society for aiding deserving slaves and slave children to purchase their freedom', founded in June 1828 by a group of worthy but conservative business and professional men and clergymen.[199]

The Society's office bearers set about their task with extreme caution and refused to condemn slavery for fear of giving offence. They restricted themselves to collecting funds in order to purchase 'female children between the ages of three and ten, to be apprenticed until the age of sixteen [later raised to eighteen], with such master or mistress as may be approved by the Committee'. During a five-year period they managed to alter the status of just 126 small girls of colour.

Although apprenticeship was intended as a useful prelude to free wage-labour, it seems to have been little more than an alternative form of slavery, particularly as some of the girls were indentured either to their original owners or to people connected with them. Each young apprentice was obliged to serve her employer faithfully to the best of her ability, and 'honestly, decently and obediently behave herself towards her said master and obey all his lawful commands during the said term'. In return for long hours of housework and child-minding, she was entitled to 'good and sufficient lodging, clothing, food, medical treatment and everything necessary' for her maintenance. Employers were supposed to teach their apprentices practical skills in order to prepare them to earn a future livelihood, but this was largely ignored. They were also required to 'encourage, and if necessary compel, attendance at a proper school [three times a week] and on public worship'.

Before any child could be purchased by the Society, her mother was required to declare her consent to such a sale. Purchase prices varied from ten guineas for the younger children to £25 or more for those over the age of eight. Funds accumulated slowly, but were boosted by generous donations from sympathisers in India. After transfer, the children remained the property of the Philanthropic Society until their apprenticeships expired. Reports from employers concerning illness, injury, death, disobedience or absenteeism were noted, and the Committee investigated occasional complaints of maltreatment made by concerned parents.

These were generally discounted, as may be seen from an entry in the Minute Book for April 1829:

> A written statement was submitted to the Committee from the slave Candace belonging to Mr Maasdorp, charging Mrs Norman with ill treating her child Leentje [aged 10], and stating also that she in consequence had taken away the child from Mrs Norman's service. The parties appeared before the Committee and the complaint on being investigated was found to be frivolous and groundless; the Committee were of the opinion that the slave Candace had acted in a very improper manner towards Mrs Norman, and that the child Leentje should be immediately returned to Mrs Norman's service. The Secretary was instructed to write to Mr Maasdorp with a request that he was to exercise his authority, and order the slave Candace to immediately restore the child to Mrs Norman, and to caution her against a repetition of such conduct.

It is difficult to understand how children as young as three or four could be considered suitable for apprenticeship. However, in the case of Jida, aged five and Gilima, aged about three, slave children belonging to Mr Valentijn, it was resolved that 'on account of their tender age they be allowed to remain with their mother until the committee shall think fit to apprentice them'. Today, the notion of summarily removing little girls from their families and from the security of the Dutch households where they had been born and sending them to live with strangers, including uncomprehending English immigrants, seems barbaric. Resistance was difficult, but one or two apprentices showed unexpected streaks of independence. In February 1831, Mrs Hanson complained of the misconduct of her apprentice Alemina, aged eleven and a half, who sometimes absconded for several days at a time. As she had not returned, Mrs Hanson requested the cancellation of her indentures and respectfully solicited another apprentice 'when an opportunity may offer'. The Committee agreed, and asked the police to find the missing girl and have her punished. Alemina evaded capture until the beginning of April, when she appeared in the Police Court charged with repeated desertion. She was sentenced to eight days solitary imprisonment on a spare diet.[200]

18a. Two slave employers who were not owners: JG Swaving (1784–1835), a Dutch immigrant who became interpreter and translator at the Cape Supreme Court in 1827, hired the housemaid Rachel of the Cape by the month. (Engraving of a portrait by JE Ford copied from Swaving's Tienjarige militaire loopbaan door hem zelven beschreven, *published in 1830.)*

Octavia of the Cape

It is impossible to know what forces were at work when a child named Octavia of the Cape left the land of her birth on Christmas Day 1830, and vanished. From clues in old newspapers, pamphlets and minute books it appears that she was the eldest daughter of Constantia, a slave belonging to Carel Maurits Zastron (1798 to 1845), chief clerk in the Slaves and Deeds Registry Office in Cape Town. He was of German descent, one of a number of anglicised Dutch-speaking citizens who joined the British administration. Years later, in 1851, his daughter married JH Brand, who later became president of the Orange Free State.

In June 1830, Zastron offered to sell three slave sisters to the Cape of Good Hope Philanthropic Society. He proposed that the Committee arrange apprenticeships for Octavia, aged eight, and Laura, aged six, but he wanted to have the infant Julenda, aged thirteen months, apprenticed to himself. Their mother consented, and she and the children appeared before the earnest gentlemen who ran the Society. It was

18b. Mrs Kift, formerly Carolina Petronella Heckroth (1810–80), employed the indentured slave apprentice Octavia of the Cape prior to her disappearance on Christmas Day 1830. Carolina was the grand-daughter of Adam Seidel and an emancipated slave named Regina Margaretha Lourens of the Cape. This portrait was painted in the 1850s, when the Kifts were living in Port Elizabeth.

resolved that 'a sum of £45 be offered to Mr Zastron for Octavia and Laura,' but they were not prepared to purchase Julenda until 'she shall have attained the age of three years'. Zastron held out for £52 10 shillings, and got it – a considerable capital sum in those days. A month later he sold their brother Abraham, aged 10, to G Munnik of Cape Town.

Octavia was transferred to the Society in July 1830 and apprenticed to Edmund Lombard Kift, an Irishman who had recently married Carolina Heckroth according to the rites of the English Church.[201] It is not clear whether the Kifts employed other servants, but little Octavia, who was known to them as 'Taffey', was no doubt kept busy by her new mistress, who was pregnant. On Christmas Day she was given permission to leave the Kifts' Plein Street home to accompany her mother Constantia to chapel. The agitated woman returned several hours later with the astonishing news that her daughter had been stolen away by a stranger named King, a passenger on board the *City of Edinburgh*, a British vessel that had put in for water five days earlier. The ship had left Bristol early in October bound for Calcutta, and was carrying 'sundry cargo' – and Mr and Mrs King and family.[202] By the time the authorities got wind of the kidnapping the *City of Edinburgh* had cleared Table Bay, and it was too late to rescue Octavia.[203]

The abducted apprentice was legally the property of the Society until she reached her eighteenth year, and the case was handed over to the superintendent of police. In February, the captain of the *City of Edinburgh* was charged *in absentia* with 'taking from the Colony without a colonial pass the child Octavia belonging to the Society', and Alexander Thompson, a local merchant who acted as surety for the master, was summoned to appear in court. According to evidence, the child arrived on board a few minutes prior to sailing, when the captain's attention was fully engaged in getting under weigh. There existed no proof that he was aware of the child being on board, or that the Colonial Office had not granted the requisite permission, and the case was dismissed.[204] Although the Society sought the opinion of the attorney general, no attempt was made to find and prosecute King, the man who presumably persuaded her to board a rowing boat for the short journey to the ship at anchor in the Bay.

Whether Octavia sailed away reluctantly or willingly remains a mystery. Perhaps the prospect of a foreign adventure seemed more attractive than a nine-year apprenticeship to the Kifts. She may not have realised that she was destined to become a mother's help and nursemaid to King's children, who had already been cooped up aboard ship for 70 days. Her mother seems to have raised the alarm rather late – was she duped or negligent? A month after Octavia's disappearance Zastron sold Constantia and her youngest daughter Julenda to George Twycross of Cape Town.

Having lost his youthful servant, Kift asked to be allocated 'some other child purchased by the Society' as an apprentice. This was approved, and Laura, aged six and a half, took the place of her missing sister. The words 'Left the Colony' appear next to Octavia's name in the Society's annual reports, and she apparently never returned.[205]

Emancipation and its aftermath

British immigrants like John Fairbairn, editor of the *South African Commercial Advertiser*, had long seen slavery as a hurdle to commercial enterprise, and they discussed emancipation in economic rather than philanthropic terms. Slaves represented 'money locked up' that earned no interest. Dishonest slaves and those with criminal tendencies were a liability to their owners, who were responsible for their misdemeanors. When they died they were a loss, especially if recently purchased. Taking every expense into consideration, it cost at least 13 Rixdollars a month to keep a slave and there would be no difficulty in obtaining able and energetic servants for that wage. Domestic peace would be enhanced, and owners would get rid of a world of troubles. 'No more attending magistrate's courts on the complaints of his slaves,' wrote one anonymous correspondent. 'No more paying of fines for correcting them when irritated by their misconduct. No more anxious feeling when he hears of a robbery or murder in his neighbourhood ...'[206]

Slavery ended at the Cape on 1 December 1834, but its impact was deferred because slaves were obliged to serve a compulsory 'apprenticeship' until December 1838. Even rational slave proprietors became increasingly jittery as Emancipation Day approached, but the celebrations were orderly and there were good attendances at thanksgiving services in mission churches. Slaves knew just how reluctant their owners were to abandon a system that had served them so well, and some ascribed their freedom to the direct intervention of King William IV. An illiterate slave named February of the Cape, his wife Jacoba and their children, all of Eerste River, conveyed their gratitude to Sir Benjamin D'Urban in a letter dictated to a scribe: 'We, the undersigned, beg to express to Your Excellency in Council, and request you will convey to His Majesty our King, our heartfelt thanks for the blessing of freedom lately bestowed upon us and our fellow bondsmen by His Majesty's most gracious command.'[207] They pledged their loyalty to the Crown and hoped not to disappoint the governor in his good expectations of them.

Most slaves had expected immediate emancipation and the four-year apprenticeship was a source of bitter disappointment, especially to the elderly, who dreamed of spending their last days in freedom. During this long hiccup, employers were supposed to prepare their former slaves for an independent life, but few took the injunction seriously. Farmers benefited most from the delay – urban slave owners had long been exposed to an alternative social order. Apprentices became increasingly insolent and resentful, and there were many desertions.

D'Urban has been commended for his firm leadership during the sensitive emancipation period, but an official dispatch reveals that his sympathies were firmly with the employers.[208] In 1837, he wrote to the Secretary of State for the Colonies in London, forwarding a petition from a group of Cape farmers asking that the liberation of apprentices be postponed for five months to allow the 1838/9 harvest to be gathered without disruption. He foresaw 'evil effects' if the apprentices decided to quit their employment at the most critical period of the year in order to enjoy their first moments of liberty. Should their employers tempt them to stay by offering them 'adequate wages', this would cause resentment and dissatisfaction 'pregnant with greater evils' when they discovered that these levels of remuneration were merely temporary. On the other hand, postponing the date would upset those employers who were keen to rid themselves of the burden of supporting troublesome apprentices, bluntly described by D'Urban as 'useless and depraved servants'. His sentiments were shared by farmers like AJ Louw of Koeberg, who pleaded for strict vagrancy laws to prevent ex-slaves leading a lazy and easy life. He predicted that crops would be exposed to destruction when 'thousands of untutored, mostly immoral beings, are incorporated with civil society, without proper laws to check [their] ungovernable passions'.[209]

The governor didn't know it, but his frontier policies had caused dissatisfaction in London and he was about to be replaced. On a wet day in December 1838 approximately 36 000 Cape slaves gained their freedom under the supervision of his successor, Sir George Napier, and began new lives as best they might. Celebrations were generally orderly and restrained, and the day passed without any of the disruptions that nervous inhabitants had been predicting. According to Johan George Steytler, a boy of six in 1838, the apprentices paraded in Cape Town singing a Dutch song in which every verse ended with: 'Victoria! Victoria! *Daar waai de Engelschen vlaag,*' and when his mother asked a young woman to go on an errand, she replied: 'No, I won't, we are free today!'[210] Napier wisely declined to listen to complaints by busybodies who grumbled about noise and other civic 'nuisances'.

The transition to wage labour was relatively smooth for urban apprentices, but ex-slaves who had endured callous treatment on the farms headed for the mission stations or the towns in search of better prospects. Many broken families were reunited, but some who had been forcibly separated were too poor to leave their immediate neighbourhood. Those who lacked the skills and resources to support themselves independently were forced to remain on the land, but at least they were free to choose when and where to work, and harsh taskmasters found it difficult to retain labour.

In March 1839 Fanny Parkes, a lively Englishwoman with an insatiable curiosity, arrived at the Cape from India, en route to England.[211] Her stay included the almost obligatory visit to a Constantia wine farm, where Mrs van Reenen complained greatly of the emancipation of the slaves. Some of them were unwilling to be free, while others rejoiced that freedom had procured them idleness. 'Their wages being high and food cheap, the emancipated people will only work now and then. The slaves collect in Cape Town, they work for a week, the wages of seven days will supply them with rice and fish for a [good] length of time; and until forced by necessity, they will not work again.'

When Fanny returned to the Cape in 1843 she took careful note of how poor people made a living. Although her writing displays the usual prejudices of her time and class, her remarks were based on personal observation. She went to the fish market, a square-walled enclosure near the old jetty, where all sorts of people were huddled together selling or buying fish.

> Cartloads of the most enormous craw-fish lay on the ground, crawling about and fighting each other; and near to them were heaps of silver-fish, and quantities of Cape salmon and fish without scales, with long thin bodies and pointed heads, which were sold for one penny each – good when salted and smoked. The porters who attend the market carry the fish away in baskets slung to each end of a long pole balanced on the shoulder. I bought a gielbeck or yellow beak, for which I paid twopence. A Malay porter carried it to the house on a stick through its gills, for which his pay was also twopence – a great price for a short distance, compared with the price of the fish, which was a *very large* one.

One day she followed the stream leading to the washing place below Platteklip Gorge.

> Hundreds of women and some few men were all employed washing clothes by beating them upon the stones in the stream; some of the women with their infants tied upon their backs ... and the whole side of the mountain was covered with linen drying on the grass. They ask four shillings and sixpence ... a dozen for washing clothes, but will generally take two shillings and sixpence. For the ship passengers they wash very badly; for people resident in Cape Town they wash well.

She also walked to Green Point to gather shells. 'The people dig for them here, and procure them in great quantities out of the sand, which they sift; they are sold to burn for lime, which is made at less cost from the shells than from the limestone quarries, as on the latter a duty is levied by the municipality.' In fine weather Fanny often rambled, sketched and botanised on the slopes of Table Mountain, where she observed people collecting the juice which flowed in great abundance from the flower of the honey bush, *Protea repens*. 'They warm it, and sell it in quart bottles at three shillings a piece to the druggists, who recommend it for coughs.'

Picturesque, perhaps, but a harsh hand-to-mouth existence nevertheless. There had been no attempt to create a self-sustaining peasantry by distributing vacant crown land, and poor people were expected to find some means of support without any assistance from the authorities. Artisans and tradesmen managed well enough, but the aged and infirm and those who had spent years as domestic drudges or field hands struggled to obtain regular employment. Even the most industrious ex-slaves were unable to accumulate sufficient land or capital to generate real wealth, and they were denied access to international commerce. Joumat, 40 years old in 1838, spent the next 55 years sitting under a fir tree in Church Square with his baskets about him, selling fruit. Although he displayed a certain perverse logic in choosing the very tree beneath which slave auctions had previously been held, he lived a hand-to-mouth existence and depended for warm winter clothing on the charity of a local shopkeeper. There was no large-scale industry at the Cape prior to the 1890s and the majority remained trapped in a self-perpetuating cycle of poverty, relying on the intermittent income they obtained from handicrafts, petty retailing and wage labour to support their families. Their rent money swelled the profits of white landlords, including some who used their slave compensation funds to erect dozens of cheap hire-houses in the Bo-Kaap and the area later known as District Six.

Were they disappointed to find that although freedom united many families, it did not deliver them from want? The psychological significance of the rite of emancipation should not be discounted – people of colour celebrated Emancipation Day for at least two generations, and marked its centenary with a grand pageant. Education was the key to advancement, but there were never enough places in the overcrowded mission schools, and standards of instruction were poor. The few who persevered with their studies gained the respect of the community and became the new coloured elite. For the rest, Fanny Parkes noticed that the young women were extremely fond of balls and gaieties, which they attended dressed in the brightest of colours, and she admired their innate musical talent: 'They appear to have a taste for music, judging from the correct manner in which I have heard the children singing various airs on the mountain,' she wrote.

After seventeen decades of slavery, it was enough, perhaps, to know that they were free.

Twelve

Two ex-slaves

Carel Pilgrim

Carel of the Cape, a tailor who became a teacher and then a priest, is a well-known historical figure, but his personal life has always been shadowy. Although born a slave, he became the first Cape Muslim to undertake the arduous pilgrimage to Mecca, having been encouraged to do so by the exiled Sultan of Anjouan (an island in the Comoros), who spent 18 months at the Cape in 1833 and 1834. On his return, Carel founded a congregation that met in his house in Buitengracht, and his name was sometimes mentioned in the press in connection with religious disputes and court cases. Unlike some of his fellow priests, he was never able to build a mosque or establish a priestly dynasty.

The first surprise was his death notice, made out in the name of 'Hadjie Gazadien Carel Pelgrim' and signed by his eldest daughter Fatima in 1863.[212] This revealed that Carel was the illegitimate son of a Christian father, [Jan] Gottlieb Barends, and Pakka, a slave. Similar information appears on his brother Philip's death notice.[213] It has not been possible to establish exactly when Carel was born. His death notice states he was 85 when he died, which gives him a birth date of 1778, but this may be several years too early. He indicated a date of 1790 when he gave evidence in court in 1850, but that would have made him 13 years younger than his first wife Japoera, which seems unlikely. Somewhere in the region of 1785 may be nearer the mark.

Gottlieb Barends, a German immigrant, married a woman of colour in 1758 and died in 1784. His eldest son Johan Gottlieb – known as Jan – was illegitimate. Jan appears to have had children by two different women of colour in the 1780s: Jamilia of the Cape, a free woman whose son was baptised in 1783, and a slave named Pakka whose children Carel and Philip inherited her status. She and her sons are mentioned in a notarial protocol drawn up in 1801, when they were transferred to a burgher named Cornelis van der Poel.[214] When the latter died in 1804, he made provision in his will for the manumission of Pakka and Carel, subject to certain conditions.

Many Muslim ex-slaves discarded their slave names when they obtained their freedom and substituted Islamic names. 'Hassan al-Din', the name adopted by Carel, appears in local records in about a dozen different variations, including Gasmodien, Gastordien and Gasnodien, but he preferred to sign himself 'Carel Pelgrim'. As a teacher of Arabic, he must have studied under one of the early teachers, possibly Jan of Bougies or Achmat of Bengal. The fact that he could also sign his name in the European manner shows a high level of intelligence and literacy.

What of his mother Pakka? The most likely candidate seems to be Janpakka of Batavia (*c.*1755 to 1835), who kept a retail shop in the Waterkant in the 1820s, but her death notice lists two daughters and does not mention either Carel or Philip.[215] However, the name Gazandien occurs among the descendants of her daughter Jaria, who married a priest named Abo Raffie and settled in Port Elizabeth. Death notices, where they exist, are sometimes extremely unreliable, particularly in the cases where the deceased was elderly. The printed forms were generally completed by third parties acting on behalf of illiterate relatives, whose knowledge of their forebears was based solely on oral tradition. Disappointing as they are, they are often the only source of biographical information available for people of colour.

The directories list Carel van de Kaap as a free tailor living in Hout Street in 1816 and as a Malay schoolmaster in 1830. His brother Philip (1789 to 1844), also a tailor, was not a practicing Muslim. Some of his children were baptised, and in 1838 he married their mother, Carolina Marteyn of the Cape, in the Dutch Reformed Church.

Once free, Carel prospered. In 1817, he loaned Seymen of the Cape 600 Rixdollars to enable him to free his slave daughter Cananga, and in 1822 he bought his own home in Matfeld Lane. In October 1833, he and his wife made a joint will in which they are described as the free man Carel of the Cape, alias Gaszimoedien, formerly a tailor, now a teacher in the Arabic language, and Johanna Salomonse, alias Japoera, born at the Cape.[216] She seems to have been an exemplary Muslim wife, and Carel held her in high esteem. He set out for Mecca soon afterwards, and her encouragement must have been crucial to the success of his pioneering journey.

Carel's pilgrimage probably included periods of study and discussion, and he may have been away for up to three years – an indication of spiritual dedication and above-average wealth. On his return, he established his own congregation and mortgaged two of his houses for £600 in order to purchase a large corner property in Buitengracht that had sufficient space for a prayer room. The 1840s started promisingly enough, but before the decade ended Carel had become embroiled in a religious dispute, buried three wives and been declared insolvent.

Japoera, who was childless, died in the big house in Buitengracht early in 1841.[217] Their union must have been particularly close, for on 27 January, Carel published the following notice in the South African Commercial Advertiser in English and Dutch: 'The Heavenly Father, Lord of life and death, was pleased, on the 16th instant, to call from me my beloved wife Japoera, aged 64 years, 4 months and 16 days, after a happy union of [many?] years. All who knew her virtuous character will sympathize with my loss, of which I hereby give notice to friends and relatives, requesting to be excused the visits of condolence. Carel of the Cape, the first Pilgrim and Priest.'[218]

Although the chief priest at the time, Imam Achmat of Bengal, had not made the pilgrimage to Mecca, his status was secure. He was in charge of the Auwal Mosque, the older of the two mosques at the Cape, and overseer of the historic Muslim burial ground on Signal Hill, surveyed in 1830. Several other Islamic scholars had established small home-based congregations, including Abdol Roef, son of the legendary Imam Abdullah. Carel's main challenge came from Imam Samodien (1800 to 1868), another early pilgrim, whose followers met at his house in Keerom Street.

One of Samodien's elders, Magmoud, quarrelled with Rammelan, one of Carel's elders, over a wall that Rammelan had erected round a relative's grave. This case, which went to court in 1842, also involved Carel, who had constructed a wall and arch over Japoera's grave. In May of that year, Carel Pilgrim wrote to Sir George Napier explaining that he had buried his wife within the walled burial ground on the right-hand side of Longmarket Street, where others of his family also had been deposited.[219]

To his extreme horror he found on two occasions 'that certain heartless and vindictive monsters in human form have, to gratify their personal resentment towards himself, disturbed the remains of the dear deceased, and exposed them to view'. These wretches admitted committing the atrocity but claimed that as the burial ground had not been officially surveyed and transferred, 'they had the right to dig up the bodies, if it suited their pleasure'. Carel pointed out that the cemetery had been in use for 20 or 30 years and asked the governor to 'secure the repose of the dead in future from disturbance and molestation' by granting the small cemetery to 'whomsoever of the priests ... Your Excellency may deem fit'.

Hearing this, Magmoud was quick to present his side of the story.[220] He explained that he was the adopted son of the deceased priest Nuruman (also known as Paay Schaapie), who had obtained General Janssens' permission to use the site as a burial ground some four decades previously. Before his death, Nuruman had given Magmoud charge of the cemetery and instructed him in the presence of the elders to keep the boundary wall in good repair, see that the dead were properly buried in a line, and prevent the building of vaults or arches over the graves.

Magmoud had attended to this for many years, 'and everything went on very regular until of late, when the Malay priest Carel Gasmodien ... thought proper to build an arch and wall round the place where his said wife was buried'. When Carel refused to remove this edifice, the two exchanged angry words. Meanwhile, another person (presumably Rammelan) erected a wall twice the size round his brother's grave, citing

19. Carel Pilgrim, painted by the British artist George French Angas in 1847. Angas described him as an obliging and interesting man who held more liberal views than any of his rival priests. He claimed to be the original and only genuine pilgrim amongst the followers of the Prophet in Cape Town, and was always willing to discuss Muslim customs and ceremonies. He sat repeatedly for his portrait, and coffee and cakes were offered whenever the artist visited his house. (Portrait copied from The Kafirs illustrated *by Angas, published in 1849.)*

Carel's example as a precedent. Magmoud, fearing that the burial ground would soon be 'filled with walls instead of dead bodies', took it upon himself to remove both structures.

The aggrieved parties then instituted an action in the Magistrate's Court that put Magmoud, a sickly man, to considerable expense. Although he won the case, his custodianship was threatened by Carel's application for the transfer of the property. Magmoud asked to be quietly allowed to continue his work, and requested that after his death the charge devolve on his priest, Hadje Samodien, in order to prevent further misunderstandings.

The governor suspected that the dispute might simmer on for years if he showed any partiality. He therefore instructed the municipal commissioners to transfer the site to the surveyor general, to be held in trust for the whole of the Mohammedan population 'of whatsoever sect or congregation'. Rational as this decision appeared, it did not have a beneficial effect. Once custody was taken out of Muslim hands, the burial ground fell into 'a most disgraceful state'. By 1857, the walls were falling down, and no one felt inclined to pay for repairs. Hadje Samodien complained that burials were made without any order or consideration for the convenience or feelings of others, and asked to be appointed superintendent.[221] When the resident magistrate asked one of Carel Pilgrim's supporters to carry out repairs and oversee burials, five priests complained and demanded that a neutral person be appointed 'to preserve unanimity'.[222] Tensions appear to have eased after Carel's death in 1863, and Imam Nuruman's cemetery was eventually transferred to the Moslem Cemetery Board in 1934.

Carel Pilgrim does not appear to have resumed tailoring upon his return to Cape Town. Instead, he became a landlord, renting out houses, rooms, stores and cellars, and he pledged some of his bonded properties as security for a debt incurred by his associate Domingo, alias Abdol Wagie. His financial affairs became even more tangled in 1841 when he mortgaged his Buitengracht home for £1 000. He and Domingo subsequently raised more capital by means of several smaller interlinked mortgages that they could not service.[223] They were both sued in the Supreme Court during the 1840s, and were later declared insolvent.[224]

In August 1848, three of Carel Pilgrim's houses were offered for sale by his sequestrator. They all realised less than their mortgaged value, and there was a shortfall of more than £1 000 owing to his creditors. In 1850 he wrote to the governor, Sir Harry Smith, explaining that he was the owner of several houses in Cape Town, but, having got into difficulties, all his property, including his place of worship, had been sold.[225] Through the kindness of his creditors he had been allowed to retain a certain house in Castle Street for the sum of £450, on condition that he should pass a bond for the full sum.

Carel pointed out that as the house was part of his insolvent estate, it would have to be transferred back to him to enable him to raise a bond,

and he pleaded that it would be a hardship to be obliged to pay transfer dues on his own house at a time when he possessed 'no pecuniary means whatsoever'. There was no precedent for such a request, but William Porter, the learned attorney general, decided that his application was reasonable, and it was granted.

This must have been a difficult time for the aging priest, who was one of relatively few Cape Muslims to practice polygamy. His young wife Saartje died in 1848, followed by his spouse Nasia in 1849.[226] It is not known when he married Nasia, who was painted by the visiting British artist George French Angas in 1847, but she and Saartje were certainly co-wives, and she willed her possessions to Saartje's minor children.[227] .

In 1851, Carel was too impoverished to purchase Saartje's fine four poster bedstead and other furniture, and this had to be sold to settle her deceased estate.[228] A cedarwood wardrobe and some domestic items were set aside for her children Fatima and Achmat, including pots, kettles, a tart pan and some crockery and cutlery. Her three dresses, one rose, one

20. The lower part of the Bo-Kaap as Carel Pilgrim would have known it. This view down Chiappini Street towards Table Bay was taken before the opening of the Alfred Dock in 1867. The church-like building above the street is the Jamia Mosque, the fourth (and largest) to be opened in Cape Town. It was a purpose-built mosque – unlike the others, which were converted dwellings – and it had no minaret when it was inaugurated by the Muslim priest Abdol Bazier in 1852.

green and one velvet, and her shifts, shawls, nightgowns, petticoats and finger rings, all carefully listed, are poignant reminders that she was only 26 when she died. Her executor, Damon (alias Abadia), asked nothing for his trouble, saying that it was against his religion to charge for assisting 'poor orphans'.

Carel spent the last years of his life with his fourth wife Fatima and their five young children, and she survived him by almost 30 years.[229] According to the *Post Office Directory* for 1855, the family continued to live at 17 Buitengracht, perhaps renting the portion of his former home that contained his place of worship. This large corner property had a lower section and three entrances. It was home to a total of 53 people, including a wheelwright, a sailmaker, a fish curer, several labourers, servants and coolies, and all their children. Two of the tenants were Portuguese and the rest seem to have been people of colour.

In the nineteenth century, Cape imams provided a variety of services, including spiritual and temporal leadership, religious instruction and medical treatment. Their followers valued their medical knowledge, passed down by Eastern slaves and detainees who understood the healing properties of plants and herbs, and were strengthened by their mystical beliefs and prayers. However, levels of expertise varied considerably, and their detractors insisted that they were all skillful poisoners. Blind to the inadequacies of their own science, western doctors ridiculed the idea that Muslim holy men could cure disease. Although the era of ruthless barber-surgeons had passed, many white patients had to endure the application of leeches, purgatives and emetics that delayed, rather than hastened, their recovery.

In 1839, shortly after Carel Pilgrim returned from pilgrimage, 15 000 Capetonians – three-fifths of the population – were infected by a 'mild' strain of measles, and about 150 died, mainly children. A public hospital was set up in the redundant 'new' Slave Lodge (where UCT's Hiddingh Hall property is today), but most poor people stayed away and relied on salts, senna leaves and traditional remedies. The death notices for the year make dismal reading. Kafora and October lost their twins, aged four, and Edries of the Cape, a widower, lost one-year-old Gasila, the youngest of his four small children. He had deposited £3-15s for her in the new Savings Bank, and he had to apply to have it released so that he could pay her funeral expenses. Her sister Jedah (8) died the following year during a devastating smallpox epidemic that claimed about 2 500 victims.

Carel Pilgrim had one of the smaller congregations – no more than 126 men, women and children in 1839 – but he undoubtedly played his part.[230] A vivid picture of his medical practice occurs in a report published in the *Cape Town Mail* in August 1850, concerning a dispute between the priest and a widow named Rabea about her husband's last rites. Abdol Rajab (1825 to 1850), a young cooper who lived in Brandsteeg, was Carel Pilgrim's brother-in-law.[231] He was also an office-bearer in his congregation, and when he suffered an injury, his sister asked the priest to visit him.

Carel later stated:

> I went there and saw him. He was groaning from pain. I asked what was the matter with him, and [his wife] explained that he had hurt himself. I asked her to put my hand upon the part that was injured, and she did so. I then advised her to roast an egg and to rub the part with the juice of it. The following day I again went to see him, and found him worse. I had some pomegranate rind with me, which I ordered to be boiled and the water of it I gave him to drink, but he could only swallow it with difficulty. On the Friday night following I again went there, and saw that he was going to die; I then called for the book and prayed for him, and then went away.[232]

As Abdol Rajab's condition deteriorated, Rabea became increasingly anxious about his funeral: 'The day before his death, I asked my husband what was to be done with his body after his death, but he gave me no answer; he could not speak for weakness.' After he died there was an unseemly tussle between the widow and the congregation about the form his burial should take. Rabea wanted the priest to bury him from her house, but Carel Pilgrim declared that he must be buried out of his 'church' in Buitengracht.

Neither would give way, and eventually the dead man's relatives invaded Rabea's accommodation, removed the corpse and carried it to the priest's house on a bier. The resulting uproar came to the attention of the police, and the contending parties were brought to court.[233] The hearing caused considerable excitement in the Muslim community, and charges of assault and public violence brought against Carel Pilgrim and nine others were later dropped.[234] According to a press report, the dispute revealed 'the peculiar state of society which exists among some thousands of our fellow townsmen, who have their own customs, laws, and tenets, and form a sort of oriental republic ... in the midst of our European civilisation'.[235]

The 1860s were years of recession, and when Carel died in 1863 there was little for his family to inherit, apart from his clothes, for which his sons drew lots.[236] He left his books to his followers, but there are no indications that his congregation survived. There were already five mosques in the Bo-Kaap, and some local Muslims were beginning to look to the Sultan of Turkey for spiritual leadership. Carel's insolvency probably blighted his sons' prospects, and they were in any case too young and inexperienced to succeed him.

His descendants have left few archival footprints, apart from Abdulla Gasnodien (1853 to 1920), who was ten when his father died. He was a mason who married a well-to-do woman named Kahira Arnold of Stellenbosch, the granddaughter of Simon Arnold of Batavia (1757 to 1850).[237] Both were *hadjies*, and their four children were the grandchildren of the remarkable slave, born at the Cape more than two centuries ago, who pioneered the route to Mecca.

Manisa of the Cape

In April 1914, an account by Judith Cuthbert of a rare interview with an elderly ex-slave appeared in the *Cape Times Weekly*.[238] Manisa's reminiscences include valuable information about slave punishments, and her story complements those of Emilie Lehn and the Cape wet-nurse Katie Jacobs.

Manisa, aged 89, was living in retirement in Stellenbosch at the time of the interview. After passing through a courtyard containing various farmyard animals, a dog, some cats and a monkey, Ms Cuthbert came to a small gate that opened on to a long row of rooms, each with its stable door and tiny flower garden. The rooms had originally been slave quarters, and similar accommodation could be found behind several old houses in the town. Manisa's dwelling was distinguished by a vine trellis and an overflowing garden filled with plants grown from slips.

She was proud of her horticultural skills, and said: 'Very few have such a hand as mine for making things grow. You have come just in time to see my biggest bush before it goes to my daughter. I long promised that on my death it should be hers, but I have grown weary of her saying, "Ach, Ma, I must wait so long for my Daphne tree" ... so I told her, "There child, don't long for my death: take the Daphne and let me live".'

The stable door swung open to reveal a scrupulously clean room with an earthen floor. It contained a large round table groaning under wool mats, gaily coloured vases, and shell boxes, a plain deal table and chairs, a workbasket of mending, a great canopied double bed with a snowy counterpane, sheets and lace-trimmed pillows, and two truckle beds partially screened from the rest of the room by a calico-covered frame. The walls were decorated with numerous almanacs and coloured pictures.

The truckle beds were occupied by Manisa and a grandchild who came to keep her company at night. The canopied bed was for times of sickness and death, so that people could see that she had good household effects and knew how to use them. The two women sat at the deal table, and Manisa patched sheets while she spoke of her life as a slave. When her testimony was checked against the Slave Registers and other archival documents it emerged that she – or her interviewer – had made a few errors. She was actually four years younger than she imagined, but the main thrust of her story is straightforward and has the ring of truth.

Manisa was born in September 1824 on the farm Babylon's Tooren at Groot Drakenstein, near the ruins of the first Huguenot church. The property belonged to a wealthy widow named Johanna Barbara van Biljon (1739 to 1831), the second wife of Petrus Johannes de Villiers (1741 to 1784), who is believed to have improved the homestead on Babylon's Tooren in 1777. Their marriage was brief, and Johanna Barbara married again in 1787. Her second husband, a Dutch surgeon named Cornelis Ernestus Ponty (1754 to 1814), who was fifteen years her junior, also predeceased her. The widow Ponty was the custodian of two fine farms, several loan places, a good deal of superior furniture and 61 slaves, including Manisa's parents Jeck of Mozambique and Lea of the Cape.[239] Her wealth was destined for her five step-daughters, the children of Petrus de Villiers from his first marriage.

Here Manisa's story goes astray, for she describes Ponty, whom Judith Cuthbert calls Poutet, as a kindly and even-tempered man who was attached to her mother Lea, his former ayah or nursemaid. This is plainly impossible, for Lea was 30 years younger than Ponty, who died – childless – a decade before Manisa's birth.[240] According to Manisa, his wife was very strict, and her female slaves lived in dread of her displeasure.

What seems more likely is that Johanna Barbara, who was 85 when Manisa was born, ran her estates with the help of one of her first husband's relatives – a son-in-law or more probably a grandson – who may well have been nursed by Lea. Whoever he was, he had a soft spot for the slave and never sent any of her children to the whipping post. His benevolence could not shield young Manisa from her mistress's wrath when her tasks were not done properly. His old nurse used to implore him to intercede, but he would shake his head and say: 'Ayah, let it be, if not this, it will be the other thing – I cannot save her.' The usual punishment, and the one she dreaded most, was being sent to herd the cattle in the thick bush of the foothills. The animals were difficult to manage, and she was inexperienced and frightened. She made friends with an ancient Khoi man who lived among the rocks, and he taught her how to keep the beasts together and take them to water. He sometimes drove them nearly home for her, but never let himself be seen. After reaching the house, her mistress made the tired little girl perform all her usual daily tasks.

It seems unlikely that this martinet was the extremely elderly widow Ponty, and one must suppose that there was a substitute mistress or housekeeper. Manisa's duties sound rather drastic for a child of her tender years, and she may have shared the punishments imposed on her older siblings or comrades, or perhaps she was recounting stories she heard from her mother.

There were still plenty of wild animals in the district, including grysbok and large baboons, but they did not trouble her if she had a companion or a dog with her. The large slave contingent at Babylon's Tooren might have posed a security risk, but their owners kept them in check by ensuring that they were too frightened to go abroad at night. According to Manisa, they were all afraid of 'jackals, wolves and tigers', and mad terror would seize any slave who had to leave his quarters after dark. Thinking back, she commented: 'Ach! No, the slave time was not good!'

Johanna Barbara died in November 1831, aged 92, and her slaves were dispersed. Manisa's elder sister had contracted an unofficial marriage with a slave on a neighbouring farm, and she was bought by his owner, but the rest of the family were transferred to WA Marais, one of the heirs, in 1832. Twelve months later Jeck (46), Lea (48), Marthinus (10), Manisa (8), and Lydia (4) were bought at a public sale by Johannes Jacobus Haupt (1805 to 1847) of Moddergat, a grandson of Petrus de Villiers.[241]

Manisa's memories of the sale were still vivid more than 80 years later. The auctioneer told her to jump up lightly onto the stable, hold her head up and stand straight, so that the people could see that she was worth buying. This 'poor little bundle of living merchandise' found Mynheer Haupt to be a kind master. She became an inside servant, received food from the table and was never sent to the whipping tree, as 'he was the only master in the countryside who did not thrash his slaves'.

Her new mistress died, and her owner hired her out to an old lady in Stellenbosch, who, after the work was done in the mornings, sent her little slave to the sewing school for young white ladies in the afternoons. Although Manisa was told to sit on the floor in the corner, she received just as much attention as the others. She was very grateful for this opportunity, and her patching, darning and incessant industry bore witness to her skill. 'Our mistresses made us sew; it isn't like the present days when no one sits with needlework in front of their doors, and are content with second-hand grand clothes on top, and rags underneath.'

On her master's remarriage she went back to Moddergat, and again secured an unusual advantage. A delicate young lady, the daughter of a Moravian missionary, came for a change of scene, and Manisa had to wait on her and sleep on the floor of her room. Each night, before they slept, she told Manisa about God and taught her how to pray. Her mistress would have been furious if she had known, because 'we were only animals in her sight; and I kept secret that I had learnt about God, but I didn't forget'.

She recalled:

> No, the slave days were not good. Women were put in the stocks and were also punished by having heavy leather ear-pads, just like the blinkers used for horses, tied over their ears. Ach! the whipping tree was awful; whether it was the father, mother, sister or brother or child, you had to help tie them up. The body was bare and they would be beaten until they leapt in the air, and the blood spurted out.
>
> After the slaves were freed, the apprentice system came in, and you were then sent with a note to the nearest landdrost, who was supposed to hear both sides, but most of us found they thrashed us there without bothering to hear if we were in the right or the wrong, and then we had to make up our work when we got back to the farm; so we rather let the master whip us and say nothing about it; only after a bit we would hire ourselves to a good baas; and that's where it was good to be free.
>
> We were not allowed to get married, but a male slave would ask permission from his owner and from the woman's master if he could take her, and he then slept at the woman's place without being afraid of being shot. The children of such a union always became the property of the woman's master. Females were supplied with a one-piece garment three times a year, made of quilted gingham, very like bed ticking, and the men with a jacket and trousers of leather twice a year. The smart boys used to get us to wash their leather suits with yellow sorrel blossom to make them a yellow colour.
>
> The food was very scarce, mostly soup made from either beans, mealies, potato or pumpkin. Now and again an offal (sheep's head, tripe and trotters) was given, and had to be divided between seven. A trotter and a bit of pens (tripe) and two ladles of broth for four, and the head and remaining broth for the other three. At Moddergat we didn't really suffer much from want of food, but many of us first had to steal to keep body and soul together.

Manisa, one of 18 slaves owned by Haupt, was ten years old when slavery came to an end, but she had to serve another four years as an unpaid apprentice, and in 1835 she was valued at £75 for purposes of compensation.[242] One stormy day when she was 14, Haupt came into the kitchen, called the three maidservants together, and told them they were free. 'We did not know what that meant, and so the master let us stay and fed us until we either got new places or were taken on by him as paid servants.'

After a month her mother, who had been freed earlier on account of her increasing blindness, came to fetch Manisa. 'She had walked round the district, led by my youngest sister, until she found us all, my father included, and then we were all taken into service on the farm Bottelary, where she had been living.'

After emancipation, Christian missionaries sought converts among the ex-slaves, and a year or two later large batches of up to 50 couples were baptised and married. Most had been living together for years. Manisa chuckled as she remembered the rows of dark faces, her parents included, 'clustered as closely as a wreath' round the pulpit, the brides in white calico dresses. The church was packed with their mostly grown up offspring, and it was a great day for all concerned. She was baptised 'Anna' at one of these wholesale ceremonies.

After she had adjusted to the new conditions, Manisa re-entered the service of the Haupt family in Stellenbosch, and was their housekeeper for many years, sometimes having complete charge of all their valuables. In return, the family took care of her in her old age. She remembered a smallpox epidemic wreaking fearful havoc among the coloured people of Stellenbosch. The magistrate ordered that whenever a funeral passed, bystanders should run away, holding cloths over their mouths. Everyone was terrified, and many people 'got it from fright'. Manisa knew very little about her antecedents. Her mother had kept a book that contained the dates of her children's births and where their father came from, but it was lost in a fire, despite strenuous efforts to save it. Her father always spoke of being an *uitlander*, and although Manisa thought he was a Batavian slave, the records show that he came from Mozambique. Of her own family of nine, only three survived, and they were scattered.

When she was interviewed in 1914, she was the last member of the Rhenish Church to wear the thin, soft muslin 'doek' tied tightly round her head, with no fancy folds. This 'modest and decent covering' was the regulation slave headdress, and she had no intention of changing it for a kappie or a hat. She was ill at the time of her 89th birthday, and took to her canopied bed, but she was touchingly grateful for the gifts she received, including a little good port wine from her old mistress, and an iced cake from her interviewer. 'Toch! Now I have something to offer my visitors even like other years.'

She had been allowed to retain her large room in recognition of her loyal service, and her old mistress's grandchildren sometimes gave her a helping hand. 'Ach! it makes me ashamed when they run and carry the water for me, and even one of the little ones hung out my washing today. I am not allowed to walk outside now, but sometimes I am disobedient, and I must have things clean, but they are afraid I will fall ...'

Ms Cuthbert was impressed by her loyalty, honesty, thrift and industry. Despite the evils she had experienced as a child, Manisa believed that her life had been blessed, and she looked forward confidently to 'the freedom of death'.

In the past, popular perceptions of slavery have been clouded by amnesia and denial. Those whose ancestors owned slaves have persisted in portraying them as kindly and protective, despite convincing evidence to the contrary. Slave descendants, demoralised by apartheid's demeaning mythology, have viewed their heritage as a matter for shame and concealment. This is in contrast to the descendents of north American slaves, who proudly call themselves African-Americans and celebrate their painful past in many different ways, not least through the enduring legacy of their music. They have founded churches, universities and schools, developed historic sites and slave routes, published academic and popular studies, and made contact with other communities who share a common experience of bondage. Although Australia never experienced slavery, it was colonised by reluctant British convicts who had been sentenced to transportation for a variety of crimes. After years of denying their heritage, Australians now take pride in this chapter of their history, and the search for convict ancestors is reported to have become a cottage industry.

Despite a trickle of articles about individual Cape slaves, no fleshed-out biography has yet appeared in English. This is bound to change as increasing numbers of South Africans begin to research their slave ancestors, but in the meantime, Emilie and Hans Lehn, Steyntje Smit, Carel Pilgrim and Manisa are worthy representatives of the multitudes of stalwart men and caring women who managed to survive the degradation of slavery with dignity, integrity and optimism.

21. Manisa of the Cape, aged 89, posing outside what were originally slave quarters in the village of Stellenbosch. She was the daughter of Jeck of Mozambique and Lea of the Cape, slaves of the widow Ponty of Babylon's Tooren, Groot Drakenstein.

Endnotes

This list identifies all the archival documents, newspapers and journals consulted during the preparation of *Echoes of Slavery*. To avoid peppering the text with still more numbers, references to quotations from printed travellers' accounts have been kept to a minimum.

Genealogical information has been gleaned from the standard sources, including De Villiers & Pama, Heese, Hoge, Philip, *SA Genealogies* and the *Dictionary of SA Biography.*

I must acknowledge a deep debt of gratitude to the authors, living and dead, whose works appear in the select bibliography.

Abbreviations:

AG	Attorney General
CAR	Cape Town Archives Repository
CJ	Court of Justice
CO	Colonial Office
CSC	Cape Supreme Court
GH	Government House
MOIB	Master's Office: Insolvency Branch
MOOC	Master of the Orphan Chamber
NLSA	National Library of South Africa (Cape Town Division)
SO	Slave Office

Chapter 1

1 Quotations are from Kindersley, Jemima: *Letters from the island of Teneriffe, Brazil, the Cape of Good Hope and the East Indies* (London: J Nourse, 1777).
2 Quotations are from *The Cape diaries of Lady Anne Barnard, 1799–1800,* ed. Margaret Lenta and Basil le Cordeur. 2 vols. (Cape Town: Van Riebeeck Society, 1999).
3 Immelman, Rene: ' 'n Oosterling aan die Kaap in 1799', *Die Huisgenoot,* 15.3.1935.
4 Quotations are from Abu Talib ibn Muhammad Khan: *The voyages of Mirza Abu Taleb Khan in Asia, Africa and Europe* (London: Longman, Hirst, & Orme, 1810).
5 Malan, Antonia: 'Beneath the surface – behind the doors: historical archaeology of households in mid-eighteenth century Cape Town', *Social Dynamics* 24(1) (1998), p. 98.
6 *South African Chronicle and Mercantile Advertiser,* 9.3.1825; 16.3.1825; 23.8.1825; 13.12.1825; 28.2.1826; 1.8.1826; 12.9.1826; 19.12.1826.
7 CAR: CSC 1/1/1/3 no.9. Criminal Session, August 1830.
8 CAR: CO 3949 no.218; CO 3947 no.33.
9 CAR: CO 3949 no.215.
10 CAR: CO 3953 no.61.
11 CAR: MOOC 6/9/128 no. 5512.
12 CAR: MOOC 6/9/120 no.3795.

Chapter 2

13 *South African Illustrated News,* 26.4.1884.
14 Krauss, Ferdinand: 'A description of Cape Town and its way of life, 1838–40', *Quarterly Bulletin of the South African Library* 21(1–2) (1966), p.9.
15 *South African Illustrated News,* 3.5.1884.
16 Ibid.
17 Quotations are from *The journal of Joseph Tindall, missionary in South West Africa 1839–55;* ed. BA Tindall (Cape Town: Van Riebeeck Society, 1959).

Chapter 3

18 Elizabeth Grzymala Jordan: personal communication.
19 Quotations are from: *James Ewart's Journal, covering his stay at the Cape of Good Hope (1811–1814)* (Cape Town: C Struik, 1970). pp.22; 28.
20 Abu Talib ibn Muhammad Khan: *The voyages of Mirza Abu Taleb Khan in Asia, Africa and Europe* (London: Longman, Hirst, & Orme, 1810), p.68.
21 *South African Commercial Advertiser,* 13.4.1831.
22 CAR: SO 6/30 folio 96.
23 CAR: CO 3953 no.110.

Chapter 4

24 Quotations are from Campbell, John: *Travels in South Africa;* fascim. ed. (Cape Town: Struik, 1974).
25 For her biography, see Schoeman, Karel: *Dogter van Sion; Machtelt Smit en die 18de-eeuse samelewing aan die Kaap, 1747–1799* (Kaapstad, Human & Rosseau, 1997).
26 For Bakker's life as a missionary, see *Dagboek en brieven van Mewes Jans Bakker;* ed. AH Huussen and SBI Veltkamp-Visser (Amsterdam: SA Instituut, 1991).
27 Quotations are from Teenstra, Marten Douwe: *De vruchten mijner werkzaamheden* (Cape Town: Van Riebeeck Society, 1943).

Chapter 5

28 CAR: CJ 797 no. 30.
29 CAR: CJ 797 no.45.
30 CAR: CJ 813 no.12.
31 CAR: CO 3918 no.273.
32 CAR: SO 6/135 folio 6–7; SO 6/138 folio 62.
33 CAR: CO 3891 no.695; CO 3903 no.108.
34 CAR: CO 3867 no.43; CO 3868 no.128.
35 CAR: CO 3876 no.192; CO 3881 no.11; CO 3881 no.22; CO 3885 no.44; CO 3885 no.46; CO 3885 no.61.
36 CAR: CO 3885 no.17.
37 CAR: CO 3885 no.43; CO 3885 no.32.
38 CAR: CO 3887 no.87.
39 CAR: MOOC 7/1/52 no.29.
40 CAR: CO 3860 no.625.
41 CAR: CO 3868 no.173 (second petition).
42 CAR: MOOC 7/1/69 no.22–4.
43 McMagh, Patricia: *The three Lieschings, their times and contribution to Cape medicine, 1800–1843* (Cape Town, Society for the History of Pharmacy in South Africa, 1992), p. 97.
44 CAR: CO 3898 no.15.
45 CAR: SO 6/115 folio 11.
46 CAR: CO 3898 no.11.
47 CAR: CO 3910 no.241; SO 6/12 folio 44.
48 CAR: MOOC 6/9/169 no. 6725.
49 CAR: MOOC 6/9/1 no.100; MOOC 13/1/98 no.28.
50 CAR: CO 3935 no.88.
51 CAR SO 6/13 folio 156.
52 CAR: MOOC 6/9/78 no.4363.
53 CAR: CO 3961 no.18.
54 CAR: SO 6/30 folio 138.
55 CAR: CO 3966 no.129.
56 CAR: CO 3962 no.76.

57 *South African Commercial Advertiser*, 5.2.1834.
58 CAR: SO 6/22 folio 144.
59 According to an item in the *South African Commercial Advertiser* of 13.4.1831, Thomas Alexander Christie was remanded for reportedly threatening the life of his father John.
60 CAR: CO 3950 no.133.
61 *Cape Town Gazette*, 9.6.1831.
62 CAR: SO 6/21 folio 208.

Chapter 6

63 CAR: 1/CT 16/24 (Police Office Letter Book), 10.9.1839.
64 Quotations are from *The Cape diary of Bishop Patrick Raymond Griffith for the years 1837 to 1839* (Pretoria: Southern African Catholic Bishops Conference, 1988).
65 CAR: MOOC 7/1/53 no.66.
66 CAR: SO 6/12, folio 15.
67 CAR: CO 3949 no.55.
68 CAR: SO 12/10 contains their declaration, dated 17.9.1830.
69 *South African Commercial Advertiser*, 25.2.1834.
70 CAR: MOIB 2/502 no.1.
71 CAR: CO 4018 no.547.
72 CAR: CO 3870 no.326.
73 CAR: CJ 803 no.20.
74 CAR: CO 3873 no.404.
75 CAR: CO 3876 no.194.
76 CAR: CO 3895 no.344.
77 CAR: CO 3920 no.119.
78 CAR: SO 6/23 folio 16.

Chapter 7

79 CAR: MOOC 6/9/4 no.755.
80 CAR: GH 48/2/23, pp.1-321. Much of the information in this section has been drawn from Harms' suits on Francina's behalf.
81 CAR: MOOC 6/9/49 no.431.
82 CAR: CO 3861 no.112.
83 CAR: MOOC 6/9/44 no.9284; MOOC 6/9/46 no.9760.
84 CAR: CO 3902 no.40.
85 Harms owned four adult slaves in the 1830s – a baker, a groom and two housemaids – and five children (SO 6/22 folio 43).
86 CAR: CO 3902 no.40.
87 CAR: AG 48 (Fiscal's Day Book), 4.12.1815.
88 CAR CO 3902 no.40.
89 CAR: SO 6/107 folio 123.
90 CAR: CO 3917 no.15; SO 12/3, Deeds no. 233 & 234.

91 CAR: SO 6/24 folio 76.
92 CAR: SO 6/33 folio 76. At the same time Harms purchased a slave named Roos, probably Steyn's daughter, from De Vos's son Philip Wouter de Vos of Stellenbosch, who neglected to repay the sum for which she had been mortgaged. She was detained in slavery until February 1830, when the Guardian of Slaves threatened to prosecute De Vos for failing to settle this debt (SO 2/11 pp.473–4; S0 6/107 folio 2).
93 CAR: SO 10/6 Deed no. 5706, 24.11.1827; SO 12/6, 27.11.1827.
94 CAR: MOOC 6/9/4 no.755.

Chapter 8

95 CAR: CO 3957 no.69.
96 *South African Commercial Advertiser*, 6.11.1830.
97 *South African Commercial Advertiser*, 25.5.1831.
98 *South African Commercial Advertiser*, 18.6.1831; 13.4.1831.
99 *South African Commercial Advertiser*, 26.2.1831.
100 *South African Commercial Advertiser*, 23.11.1831.
101 Quotations are from Broadbent, Samuel: *A narrative of the first introduction of Christianity amongst the Barolong tribe of the Bechuanas, South Africa* (London: Wesleyan Mission House, 1865).
102 CAR: CO 3961 no.117.
103 CAR: CJ 809 pp.437–443.
104 CAR: CO 3905 no.204.
105 CAR: CJ 810 no.13; CJ 815 no.16; CJ 817 no.5.
106 CAR: CJ 514–6. Most of the information in this section has been drawn from these detailed court records.
107 CAR: MOOC 6/9/7 no.1243.
108 CAR: CO 4826, pp.7–8, 28.10.1808.
109 CAR: CO 3873 no.418.
110 CAR: CO 16 no. 59, 30.9.1809.
111 CAR: CO 11 no. 68.
112 Sources consulted for this section were Campbell, John: *Travels in South Africa;* fascim. ed. (Cape Town: Struik, 1974); Campbell, John: *Travels in South Africa ... being a narrative of a second journey in the interior of that country*; facsim. ed. (New York: Johnson Reprint Corporation, 1967) and Thompson, George: *Travels and adventures in Southern Africa*; ed. Vernon S Forbes. 2 vols. (Cape Town, Van Riebeeck Society, 1967–8).
113 CAR: SO 6/59 folio 14.
114 CAR: CO 3926 no. 73.
115 CAR: SO 12/4: Manumission no.370, 3.3.1824.
116 Tabler, EC: Addenda and corrigenda to 'Pioneers of Rhodesia', *Africana Notes and News* 17, pp.358–60.
117 CAR: CJ 819 no.9. Much of the information in this section has been drawn from these detailed court records.

118 CAR: AG 44 pp.65–6.
119 CAR: AG 44 pp.73–83.
120 CAR: CO 2669, 8.3.1825.
121 CAR: AG 44 pp.91–7.
122 CAR: AG 44 pp.161–70.
123 CAR: CO 3928 no.309.
124 CAR: AG 44 pp.163–4.
125 CAR: SO 1/7.
126 CAR: CO 3943 no.597; CO 3952 no.63.
127 CAR: CO 3959 no.93.
128 *South African Commercial Advertiser,* 23.11.1831; De *Zuid-Afrikaan,* 18.11.1831.
129 Theal, GM: *Records of the Cape Colony 31,* p.71.
130 CAR: CO 3962 no.72.
131 CAR: SO 6/13 folio 106.
132 CAR: CSC 1/1/1/6/1 no.5.
133 CAR: CO 3968 no.73.

Chapter 9

134 *The Christian Express,* 1.11.1876 p.4; 1.12.1876, pp.13–14.
135 CAR: SO 6/57 folios 3 & 17.
136 CAR: SO 6/49 folios 65 & 101.
137 CAR: SO 6/55 folio 93.
138 CAR: SO 20/9 no.2098.
139 CAR: MOOC 6/9/45 no.9554.
140 CAR: MOOC 6/9/101 no.10005.
141 *Papers relating to the manumission of Steyntje & her children* (Cape Town: George Greig, 1827). Much of the information in this section has been drawn from this pamphlet.
142 CAR: GH 48/2/40 pp.1–126.
143 CAR: CO 3917 no.91.
144 Theal, GM: *Records of the Cape Colony 13,* pp.116–7.
145 Theal, *GM: Records of the Cape Colony 14,* p.67.
146 CAR: GH 54/1 pp.310–2.
147 CAR: GH 54/3 p.11, 22.6.1822.
148 CAR: CO 3924 no.105.
149 Steyntje does not appear to have paid these manumission fees, which were abolished in 1826. Her name was not erased from the slave register until 5.1.1830, when she, Jappa, Christina and Fytje were all belatedly de-registered (SO 3/5 appendix G). There was no mention of her younger son Willem, however.
150 CAR: SO 6/30 folio 64; MOOC 6/5. Pamela died at Garden Welgelegen on 19.4.1828.
151 CAR: CSC 2/1/1/13 no.28; *South African Commercial Advertiser,* 6.1.1831.

152 CAR: CSC 2/1/1/35 no.32.
153 CAR: MOOC 6/9/36 no.7917.
154 CAR: MOOC 7/1/181 no.130–2.

Chapter 10

155 CAR: CO 3951 no.33; CO 3951 no.189; CO 3854 no.66; CO 3954 no.139.
156 CAR: CO 3957 no.97; CO 3957 no.123.
157 CAR: CO 3957 no.35.
158 CAR: CO 3969 no.5.
159 CAR: CO 3970 no.135; CO 3960 no.107.
160 CAR: CO 3962 no.75; CO 3956 no.83.
161 CAR: CO 3964 no.59.
162 CAR: CO 3972 no.151.
163 CAR: CO 3949 no.300.
164 CAR: CO 3958 no.73.
165 CAR: CO 3960 no.94.
166 CAR: SO 6/121 folio 51.
167 CAR: SO 6/102 folio 125.
168 CAR: CO 3973 no.76.
169 CAR: CSC 1/2/1/14 no.9.
170 CAR: CO 3973 no.77.
171 *South African Commercial Advertiser,* 30.7.1834; De *Zuid-Afrikaan,* 12.9.1834.
172 CAR: CO 3973 no.88.
173 Bird, J: *Annals of Natal,* vol 1. p.459.
174 CAR: SO 20/13 no.4017, p.42.
175 CAR: MOOC 6/9/53 no.673.
176 CAR: SO 6/107 folios 20 & 111.
177 CAR: 1/STB 20/94, 19.4.1830, p.137.
178 CAR: CSC 1/1/1/3/1, 2.9.1830; *South African Commercial Advertiser,* 13.10.1830.
179 CAR: CSC 1/2/1/6 no.13.
180 *South African Commercial Advertiser,* 13.10.1830.
181 CAR: CO 417 no.55, 31.12.1833.
182 CAR: CO 3975 no.26 & 27A.
183 *South African Commercial Advertiser,* 23.7.1834.
184 In 1830, he received 39 lashes for threatening his young master and others with a sickle. *South African Commercial Advertiser,* 25.12.1830.
185 CAR: CO 3991 no.28.
186 CAR: SO 20/14 no.4463.
187 CAR: SO 6/81 folios 29 & 117.
188 Fallows' career at the Cape is discussed in: Warner, Brian: *The Royal Observatory, Cape of Good Hope, 1820–1831: the founding of a colonial observatory: incorporating a biography of Fearon Fallows* (Boston: Kluwer Academic Publishers, *c.*1995).

189 CAR: SO 6/19 folio 65.
190 CAR: SO 3/21, 19.9.1826, pp.4–5.
191 CAR: SO 6/17 folios 132 & 143.
192 CAR: SO 6/15 folio 183.
193 *Africana Notes and News,* 21(7), 1975, p.296.
194 CAR: CO 3973 no.65.
195 *De Verzamelaar,* 31.10.1843.
196 *Cape Town Mail,* 10.5.1851.
197 *Standard and Mail,* 5.8.1873; *Cape Argus,* 5.8.1873.
198 *Standard and Mail,* 23.8.1873.

Chapter 11

199 NLSA: Cape of Good Hope Philanthropic Society Collection: Minute Book 1828–31 (MSB 99), 2.6.1830. Most of the information in this section has been culled from this source.
200 *South African Commercial Advertiser,* 13.4.1831.
201 CAR: MOOC 6/9/176 no.788; MOOC 6/9/196 no.6651.
202 *South African Commercial Advertiser,* 22.12.1830.
203 NLSA: Cape of Good Hope Philanthropic Society Collection: Minute Book 1828–31 (MSB 99), 5.1.1831.
204 *South African Commercial Advertiser,* 19.1.1831.
205 Cape of Good Hope Philanthropic Society. *Annual Report,* 1830–1.
206 *South African Commercial Advertiser,* 14.5.1834: letter signed 'Candid'.
207 CAR: CO 3970 no.26.
208 CAR: GH 23/11 pp.394–6, 19.9.1837.
209 *De Zuid-Afrikaan,* 3.8.1838.
210 Steytler, Johan George: 'Remembrances from 1832–1900', *Quarterly Bulletin of the South African Library,* 25(1),1970, p.25.
211 Quotations are from Parkes, Fanny: *Wanderings of a pilgrim, in search of the picturesque* (London: Pelham Richardson, 1850).

Chapter 12

212 CAR: MOOC 6/9/105 no.738.
213 CAR: MOOC 6/9/40 no.8570.
214 CAR: NCD 1/42 no.811.
215 CAR: MOOC 6/9/5 no.899; MOOC 7/1/130 no.98.
216 CAR: MOOC 7/1/161 no.72.
217 CAR: MOOC 6/9/23 no.4780.
218 *South African Commercial Advertiser,* 27.1.1841.
219 CAR: CO 4014 no.452.
220 CAR: CO 4014 no.349.
221 CAR: CO 4098 no.S91.
222 CAR: CO 4096 no.880.
223 CAR: CSC 2/2/1/73 no.45; CSC 2/2/1/79 no.39; CSC 2/2/1/86 no.16.

224 CAR: MOIB 2/714 vol 2 no.100.
225 CAR: CO 4054 no.K1.
226 CAR: MOOC 6/9/45 no.9456; MOOC 6/9/47 no.156.
227 CAR: MOOC 7/1/197 no.31.
228 CAR: MOOC 13/1/144 no.46.
229 CAR: MOOC 6/9/475 no.1610.
230 CAR: 1/CT 16/24 (*Police Office Letter Book)*, 10.9.1839.
231 CAR: MOOC 6/9/51 no.316.
232 *Cape Town Mail*, 24.8.1850.
233 *Cape Town Mail*, 17.8.1850; 24.8.1850.
234 CAR: AG 3568, Criminal Sessions, 1.11.1850, folio 2.
235 *Cape Town Mail*, 24.8.1850.
236 CAR: MOOC 7/1/270 no.14.
237 CAR: MOOC 6/9/1764 no.2681–2.
238 *Cape Times Weekly and Farmers' Record*, 17.4.1914.
239 CAR: SO 6/100 folios 8, 9, 10 & 57.
240 CAR: MOOC 6/2 p.268.
241 CAR: SO 6/88 folio 119.
242 CAR: SO 20/13 no.3886, p.27.

Select bibliography

Books and journal articles:

Abu Talib ibn Muhammad Khan: *The voyages of Mirza Abu Taleb Khan in Asia, Africa and Europe* (London: Longman, Hirst, & Orme, 1810).

African court calender (facsimile eds., 1810–26) (Cape Town: South African Library, 1981–).

Bakker, MJ: *Dagboek en brieven van Mewes Jans Bakker*; ed. AH Huussen and SBI Veltkamp-Visser (Amsterdam: SA Instituut, 1991).

Bank, Andrew: *The decline of urban slavery in Cape Town, 1806 to 1834.* (Cape Town: University of Cape Town: Centre for African Studies, 1991).

Barnard, Anne: *The Cape diaries of Lady Anne Barnard, 1799–1800*, ed. Margaret Lenta and Basil le Cordeur. 2 vols. (Cape Town: Van Riebeeck Society, 1999).

Bradlow, Edna: 'Capitalists and labourers in the post-emancipation rural Cape', *Historia* 31(1) (1986).

Bradlow, Frank R and Margaret Cairns: *The early Cape Muslims: a study of their mosques, genealogy and origins.* (Cape Town: Balkema, 1978).

Broadbent, Samuel: *A narrative of the first introduction of Christianity amongst the Barolong tribe of the Bechuanas, South Africa* (London: Wesleyan Mission House,1865).

Burrows, Edmund H: *A history of medicine in South Africa up to the end of the nineteenth century* (Cape Town: Balkema, 1958).

Campbell, John: *Travels in South Africa*; fascim. ed. (Cape Town: Struik, 1974).

Campbell, John: *Travels in South Africa, undertaken at the request of the London Missionary Society; being a narrative of a second journey in the interior of that country*; facsim. ed. (New York: Johnson Reprint Corporation, 1967).

Cape almanacs (published annually – various titles and publishers, 1827–50).

Da Costa, Yusuf and Achmat Davids: *Pages from Cape Muslim history*. (Pietermaritzburg: Shuter & Shooter, 1994).

Davids, Achmat: *The history of the Tana Baru* (Cape Town: The Committee for the Preservation of the Tana Baru, 1985).

Davids, Achmat: *The mosques of the Bo-Kaap* (Athlone: The South African Institute of Arabic and Islamic Reseach, 1980).

De Villiers, CGS: *Geslagregisters van die ou Kaapse families*, rev. by C Pama. 2 vols. (Cape Town: Balkema, 1981).

Dictionary of South African biography. 5 vols. (1968–1987).

Du Toit, Andre and Hermann Giliomee: *Afrikaner political thought: analysis and documents, 1780–1850* (Cape Town: David Philip, 1983).

Elks, Katherine: 'The police and crime in Cape Town, 1825-1850', *Kronos* 12 (1987).

Elphick, Richard and Herman Giliomee (eds.): *The shaping of South African Society, 1652–1840;* 2nd ed, (Cape Town: Maskew Miller Longman, 1989).

Ewart, James: *James Ewart's journal, covering his stay at the Cape of Good hope (1811–1814)* (Cape Town: C. Struik, 1970).

Fransen, Hans and Mary Alexander Cook: *The old buildings of the Cape* (Cape Town: Balkema, 1980).

Griffith, Patrick Raymond: *The Cape diary of Bishop Patrick Raymond Griffith for the years 1837 to 1839* (Pretoria: Southern African Catholic Bishops Conference, 1988).

Harris, Karen: 'The slave "rebellion" of 1808', *Kleio* 20, 1988.

Heese, Hans Friedreich: *Groep sonder grense: die rol en status van die gemengde bevolking aan die Kaap, 1652–1795* (Bellville: Wes-Kaaplandse Instituut vir Historiese Navorsing, 1984).

Hoge, J: *Personalia of Germans at the Cape, 1652–1806* (Archives Year Book 9, 1946).

Holman, W: *A voyage round the world* (London: Smith, Elder & Co., 1834).

Jeppie, Shamil: 'Leadership and loyalties: the Imams of nineteenth century colonial Cape Town, South Africa', *Journal of Religion in Africa* 26(2) (1996).

Kindersley, Mrs [Jemima]: *Letters from the island of Teneriffe, Brazil, the Cape of Good Hope and the East Indies* (London: J Nourse, 1777).

Krauss, Ferdinand: 'A description of Cape Town and its way of life, 1838–40', *Quarterly Bulletin of the South African Library* 21(1–2) (1966).

Laidler, PW: *A Tavern of the ocean* (Cape Town: Maskew Miller, *c.*1926).

Langham-Carter, RR: 'Queen Rebecca', *Familia* 22 (1985).

Leibbrandt, HCV: *Précis of the archives of the Cape of Good Hope: Requesten (Memorials), 1715–1806.* 5 vols. (Cape Town: Cape Times,1905–8; South African Library, 1989).

McMagh, Patricia: *The three Lieschings, their times and contribution to Cape medicine, 1800–1843* (Cape Town: Society for the History of Pharmacy in South Africa, 1992).

Mason, John Edwin: 'The slaves and their protectors: reforming resistance in a slave society, the Cape Colony 1826–1834', *Journal of Southern African Studies* 17(1), (1991).

[Parkes, Fanny]: *Wanderings of a pilgrim, in search of the picturesque* (London: Pelham Richardson, 1850).

Philip, *Peter: British residents at the Cape, 1795–1819* (Cape Town: David Philip, 1981).

Post office and general directory for 1855, comp. J Suasso de Lima (Cape Town, Van de Sandt De Villiers, 1854).

Ross, Robert: *Cape of torments; slavery and resistance in South Africa* (London: Routledge & Kegan Paul, 1983).

Ross, Robert : 'Cape Town (1750-1850): synthesis in the dialectic of continents', in *Colonial cities*; ed. Robert J Ross and Gerard J Telkamp (Dordrecht: Marthinus Nijhoff, 1985).

Ross, Robert : 'The occupations of slaves in eighteenth century Cape Town', *Studies in the History of Cape Town* 2 (1980).

Rossouw, Fransie: 'Mrs Jemima Kindersley (1741–1809): an early traveller at the Cape', *Quarterly Bulletin of the South African Library* 51(4) (1997).

Saunders, Christopher: 'Between slavery and freedom: the importation of prize Negroes to the Cape in the aftermath of emancipation', *Kronos* 9 (1984).

Saunders, Christopher: 'Liberated Africans in the Cape Colony in the first half of the nineteenth century', *International Journal of the African Historical Studies* 18(2) (1995).

Schoeman, Karel: *Dogter van Sion; Machtelt Smit en die 18de-eeuse samelewing aan die Kaap, 1747–1799* (Kaapstad: Human & Rosseau, 1997).

Shell, Robert C-H: *Children of bondage; a social history of the slave society at the Cape of Good Hope, 1652–1838* (Johannesburg: Witwatersrand University Press, 1997).

Shell, Robert C-H: 'Between Christ and Mohammed: conversion, slavery, and gender in the urban Western Cape', in *Christianity in South Africa: a political, social & cultural history;* ed. Richard Elphick and Rodney Davenport (Cape Town: David Philip, 1997).

Shell, Robert C-H: 'Islam in South Africa, 1652–1998', in *The history of Islam in South Africa*; ed. Nehemia Levtzion and Randall L Pouwels (Cape Town: David Philip, 2000).

Shell, Robert C-H: 'An oral history of a Cape wet-nurse: Katie Jacobs', *Quarterly Bulletin of the South African Library* 46(3) (1992).

Shell, Robert C-H: 'SE Hudson's "Slaves"', *Kronos* 9 (1984).

Simons, Phillida Brooke: *Cape Dutch houses and other old favourites* (Cape Town: Fernwood Press, Cape Town, 2000).

South African genealogies, vols. 1–8 (1986–).

Standard encyclopaedia of Southern Africa. 12 vols. (1970).

Steytler, JG: 'Remembrances from 1832–1900', *Quarterly Bulletin of the South African Library* 25(1) (1970).

Tayob, Abdulkader: *Islam in South Africa: mosques, imams and sermons* (Gainesville: University of Florida Press, 1999).

Teenstra, Marten Douwe: *De vruchten mijner werkzaamheden* (Cape Town: Van Riebeeck Society, 1943).

Theal, GM: *Records of the Cape Colony*, 1795–1835 (1897–1905).

Thompson, George: *Travels and adventures in Southern Africa;* ed. Vernon S. Forbes. 2 vols. (Cape Town: Van Riebeeck Society, 1967–8).

Timoney, TW: 'Cape Town's early water supplies', *Cabo* 5(4) (1993).

Tindall, Joseph: *The journal of Joseph Tindall, missionary in South West Africa 1839–55*; ed. BA Tindall (Cape Town: Van Riebeeck Society, 1959).

Van der Merwe, Floris JG: 'n Verkenning van die vryetydsbesteding onder die Maleise slawe aan die Kaap', *Suid Afrikaanse Tydskrif vir Kultuurgeskiedenis* 11(2) (1997).

Vernal, Fiona H-S: *Steyntje van de Kaap: concubinage, racial descent and manumission in the Cape Colony, 1777–1822* (Princeton: 1996).

Ward, Kerry and Nigel Worden: 'Commemorating, suppressing, and invoking Cape slavery', in *Negotiating the past: the making of memory in South Africa*; ed. Sarah Nuttall and Carli Coetzee (Cape Town: Oxford University Press, 1998).

Warner, Brian: *The Royal Observatory, Cape of Good Hope, 1820–1831: the founding of a colonial observatory: incorporating a biography of Fearon Fallows* (Boston: Kluwer Academic Publishers, *c.*1995).

Worden, Nigel Anthony: *Cape Town, the making of a city*; ed. Nigel Worden, Elizabeth van Heyningen and Vivian Bickford-Smith (Cape Town: David Philip, 1998).

Worden, Nigel Anthony and Clifton Crais (eds.): *Breaking the chains: slavery and its legacy in the nineteenth century Cape Colony* (Johannesburg: Witwatersrand University Press,1994).

Zöllner, Linda and JA Heese: *Die Berlynse sendelinge in Suid-Afrika en hul nageslag* (Pretoria: HSRC Institute for Historical Research, 1984).

Photographic credits

1. CAR MT58
2. CAR AG15693/5
3. CAR AG15689
4. CAR A2998; D3
5. CAR A3003; D8
6. CAR A3000; D5
7. CAR A3044; D41
8. CAR E5807
9. CAR M468
10. CAR A3080; D73
11. CAR A3006; D11
12. *South African almanac and directory for the year 1831* ... compiled by George Greig (Cape Town: George Greig, n.d.)
13. CAR M368
14. CAR AG15620
15. CAR M758
16. CAR L1204
17. CAR E3213

18a. Swaving, JG: *Swaving's tienjarige militaire loopbaan door hem zelven beschreven* (Dordrecht, Blussé en Van Braam, 1830)

18b. CAR AG2069

19. Angas, George French: *The Kafirs illustrated* ... (London, J Hogarth, 1849)
20. CAR E3200
21. *Cape Times Weekly* 17.4.1914

Index

B

C